THE ACCIDENTAL HISTORIAN

The Accidental Historian

TALES OF TRASH AND TREASURE

Monte Akers

TEXAS TECH UNIVERSITY PRESS

This book is typeset in Monotype Dante. The paper used in this book meets
the minimum requirements of ANSI/NISO Z39.48–1992 (R1997). ∞

Designed by Lindsay Starr

LIBRARY OF CONGRESS CATALOGING-IN-PUBLICATION DATA

Akers, Monte, 1950–
The accidental historian : tales of trash and treasure / Monte Akers.
p. cm.
Includes bibliographical references and index.

Summary: "Chronicles the author's fascination with the past, exploring little-known
incidents, episodes, and sidelights related to the Civil War, Custer's Last Stand, the
Alamo, and the career of Bonnie and Clyde, among others. Told with humor, scholarship, self-effacement, and passion, the stories both entertain and celebrate cultural
history"—Provided by publisher.

ISBN 978-0-89672-708-3 (hardcover : alk. paper)
1. United States—History—Humor. 2. United States—History–Anecdotes. 3. Akers,
Monte, 1950– 4. Historians—United States—Biography. I. Title.
E178.4.A38 2010
973—dc22
2010021556

PRINTED IN THE UNITED STATES OF AMERICA
10 11 12 13 14 15 16 17 18 / 9 8 7 6 5 4 3 2 1

TEXAS TECH UNIVERSITY PRESS
Box 41037, Lubbock, Texas 79409–1037 USA
800.832.4042 | ttup@ttu.edu | www.ttupress.org

This book is dedicated to Madison Marie Akers, whom her granddaddy considers to be perfect.

Contents

★

Acknowledgments

★

MY SINCERE APPRECIATION GOES TO KATHLEEN DAVIS NIENDORFF, my literary agent, and to the editorial staff of Texas Tech University Press, particularly Judith Keeling, Karen Medlin, and Joanna Conrad, and to Judy Alter, copy editor, plus the two "readers" for the press and the publication committee, all of whom saw merit in the manuscript and, together, made the publication of this book a reality. My particular gratitude goes to Eric Mink and to the anonymous owner of the "Jackson/Janie" braid, who not only fulfilled a personal dream but made possible the visual sharing, or completion, of a poignant anecdote of American history. The particular talent of Christopher Zaleski, of Zaleski Studio in Austin, Texas, who prepared the illustrations for publication, must not go unnoticed nor should the generosity of the various owners of photographs or copyrights who granted permission for inclusion of the same. To the "Millets," the memory of Chuck Hillsman, Bill and Carla Coleman, Charlie Sullivan, Patty/Pat/Ramrod, Sharon Nathan, Megan, and Lexy, I say thank you for the words, music, laughter, and support. To those who read the chapter about Robert E. Lee and consider it blasphemous, thank you for not resorting to gunfire, assault, stalking, or battery in response. To David McCartney, thank you for being bigger than life and simply for having been.

THE ACCIDENTAL HISTORIAN

Prologue

History is nothing more than a thin thread of what is remembered
stretched out over an ocean of what has been forgotten.

MILAN KUNDERA

The Joke, English translation by Harper Collins (1982)

WE EACH HAVE A TALE TO TELL. SOME OF US HAVE SEVERAL.
Most of mine—the ones worth repeating—deal with events out of American history with which I had some sort of close encounter. Some are humorous, some poignant, a few difficult to believe. They revolve around some of the most popular and romantic episodes and people of our past, such as the Civil War, Custer's Last Stand, the Alamo, and Bonnie and Clyde.

I'm an attorney by profession but an amateur historian by avocation. I have been attempting to romance history like an adolescent mooning over a beautiful cheerleader since before I was old enough to notice cheerleaders. Most of the close encounters came about as a result of research, interviewing witnesses, collecting artifacts, and generally immersing myself in whatever discipline or whim might bring me closer to our American past. Thirteen tales about those encounters follow.

However, from nearly fifty years of chasing, singing of, writing about, collecting pieces of, and occasionally seducing American history, I know she cannot be possessed and rarely even cornered. She'll agree to an occasional one-night stand but will not consider a marriage proposal. Still, admirers constantly seek not only to capture her but to monopolize, possess, and claim dominion over her. Historians, particularly amateurs, can be some of the most critical, anal, and jealous people in existence. Many seem to love correcting, disputing, and denigrating the historical theories and research of others as much as they love the history itself.

Accordingly, rather than present my tales as truth or the end-all/be-all of any event, rather than claim special knowledge or expertise merely because I lived some tales and uncovered some interesting information, I declare them to be trash from the very beginning. With that out of the way, perhaps readers can simply peruse these stories, smile, and enjoy them, rather than look for reasons to correct, criticize, huff, puff, or disagree.

With that said, I hope you enjoy what follows.

1

The Lakota Gauntlets

All the historical books which contain no lies are extremely tedious.
JAQUES ANATOLE FRANCOIS THIBAULT
The Crime of Sylvestre Bonnard (1881)

TEXAS CELEBRATED ITS SESQUICENTENNIAL IN 1986, AND IN LATE 1985 I got the bright idea that I would write a historical pageant about and for the county in which I was then living. That county was Freestone, located a little less than an hour east of Waco and a little more than an hour north of Huntsville, with the Trinity River and the beginning of true East Texas on its eastern boundary. The county had a rich history, and I managed to get enough folks involved in the effort that the sesquicentennial pageant turned out to be a lively affair.

In addition to having a parade in the morning and a gigantic play, or drama, on the high-school football field that evening, reminiscent of Larry McMurtry's *Texasville*, it hosted a reunion of local World War I veterans, seventeen in number, and a small Civil War re-enactment. Confederate General John Gregg had lived in the county seat, Fairfield, before the Civil War. He commanded the Texas Brigade in Lee's Army of Northern Virginia and was killed in late 1864, so there was a bona fide excuse to link the county with the "wah." I called around Central Texas to find re-enactment units willing to put on a weekend show, or farb fest, and found a few. However, the commander of one said he would bring his "battery" of artillery to the pageant only if I, in turn, would agree to join it for the purpose of filming battle scenes for the upcoming television miniseries *North South II,* based primarily on the book *Love and War* by John Jakes.

Dress up like a Civil War soldier and be in the movies? Please, oh please, throw me into that briar patch.

So, a few weeks later, after an all-night car trip, I awoke from sleeping on the ground in a field somewhere south of Natchez, Mississippi, looked around, and found myself in the middle of the War Between the States. Men and boys wearing clothes and uniforms from the 1860s were crawling out of blankets and tents, boiling coffee, leading horses to water, and cooking breakfast. The battery from Waco with whom I was traveling had arrived too late the night before to see anything in the camp and had carried our gear from a parking lot several hundred yards away, crawled under a wagon, and gone to sleep. Now, there were no automobiles, electric or telephone lines, or modern clothing to be seen. The sounds were of birds, horses, clanking metal, axes chopping wood, and human voices. I was experiencing my first "magic moment."

Warner Brothers had invited about 1,200 Civil War re-enactors for a week of filming, and we were camped in a large wilderness area that had been prepared to represent the battles of First Manassas, Sharpsburg/ Antietam, and Petersburg. The re-enactors came from all over the country and were about evenly divided between Federal and Confederate, although most brought uniforms to portray either side. The group I was with, headquartered in Waco, consisted of two cannons, each of which was served by six re-enactors, commanded by the man who owned the guns. Warner Brothers was paying each of us $50 a day and feeding us three meals a day. Owners of horses, cannons, caissons, wagons, or other large items of Civil War paraphernalia were paid extra. It was possible I had finally found my true calling.

The scene of the first two battles was relatively easy to construct, considering it consisted primarily of woods and fields. Still, there was a faux version of the Henry house, destined to be demolished for the battle scene, and a sunken road for Antietam. For Petersburg, however, the filmmaker had erected huge earthen works, similar to Forts Stedman, Gregg, Sedgwick, and others that made up the Federal and Confederate defenses during the siege of Petersburg from June 1864 to April 1865. It was slightly amazing to behold and is available for viewing in a complete DVD collection. Considering that the miniseries turned out to be extremely sappy, soap opera-ish, and cloying, one should proceed at his or her own risk.

But we didn't know at the time that the show would be cornball. What we knew was that Patrick Swayze, Parker Stevenson, Hal Holbrook, and a bouquet of lesser-known actors and actresses were being filmed while we ran, marched, battled, and died in the background. The actors were friendly and as curious about the re-enactors as we were about them. Photos were posed, autographs secured, and an adventure was had by all.

The two guns in my "battery" consisted of a Three-inch Ordinance Rifle and what is called a Wiard Gun. The former is a black rifled artillery piece nearly as familiar to battlefield visitors and movie-goers as a Napoleon cannon. The latter, while absolutely, totally correct and authentic, is less well-known. It was named for its inventor, but the phonetics fit the cannon's appearance as well. Its barrel, or tube, resembled a telescope consisting of only two sections. The front, from the muzzle back, was normal-sized, as cannons go, for about two feet, but the remaining portion, about two-thirds of the length of the gun, was twice as large in diameter. The extra thickness was intended to overcome a pesky problem involving the bursting of cannon barrels after multiple shots, but the practical effect, for Hollywood, was that it was simply too "Wiard" to be in the movies. Our gun and its crew were pulled out of the line and told we would not be in show business after all.

Rather than be crushed, I was liberated. I had, by this time, met and made a friend of Charlie Sullivan, head of the history department for Mississippi Gulf Coast Junior College in Perkiston, Mississippi. We were about the same in age, size, appearance, love of history, and alleged intellect, and, best of all, we had simultaneously become free agents in the local Civil War movie-making industry. The unit of the Mississippi artillery re-enactors he had accompanied to the filming could only stay for a weekend. Charlie and I planned to stay for the full week, so we threw in together and vowed to make an adventure of the time we had.

Unlike the other re-enactors, who were members of specific faux military units and were expected to live like faux enlisted men, noncoms, and officers, including obedience to at least a modicum of military order and routine, Charlie and I were unfettered, unattached, and undisciplined. We each possessed both Federal and Confederate uniforms, we knew that most re-enactment units welcomed additional warm bodies, and we were not shy about asking, or begging, to be allowed to join up with any unit we believed might get on camera that day. We made it our goal for the week to get filmed firing the shots that killed us.

Following a re-enactment of the Battle of First Manassas, in which we served as Confederate artillerymen, we joined a Confederate gun crew for the filming of part of the battle of Sharpsburg. Then, by borrowing a couple of extra rifles, we were allowed to join a unit of Confederate Infantry for more of Sharpsburg. At one point, a Rebel color-bearer was shot next to me, and I picked up the fallen battle flag and waved it defiantly in the face of both the advancing Yankees and, more importantly, a whirring camera.

For the last big scene—the Battle of Petersburg—we enlisted in a company of Federal engineers. That might not sound like a unit that would have potential for being filmed, but actually it was. The scene to be acted out was the Federal assault on the Confederate lines that took place on April 2, 1865, and precipitated the collapse of Lee's army and the retreat to Appomattox. The Federal engineers were to be in the vanguard of the charge.

The Confederate earthworks were protected by a trench, or moat, about eight feet deep and twenty feet wide, and Warner Brothers' concept of how Yankee attackers would have forded the ditch was to have "engineers" carry and deploy "bridges" for the infantrymen to run across.

Each bridge consisted of two sets of wooden planks that were about three feet wide and sixteen feet long. Each set was carried by eight men, who gripped the plank by means of two-by-six boards nailed perpendicular to the plank at four-foot intervals and extending about a foot and a half on each side of the plank. Thus sixteen men were needed to construct each bridge, and there were eight or ten bridges in total.

The idea was for the engineers to run forward, in advance of the infantry, under fire, carrying their plank bridges. When each team reached the trench, the first set of plank carriers was to toss one end of its plank into the moat, run down it to the bottom, then turn around and receive the second

Charles Sullivan and actor Parker Stevenson on the set of the television miniseries, *North South II* in November 1986. Portions of the Battle of Petersburg earthworks constructed for the filming appear behind them. The trench across which Sullivan and the author, portraying Federal engineers, erected foot bridges for attacking Federal soldiers to cross during the filming of the battle may be seen at right. Courtesy of the *Clarion-Ledger*, Jackson, Mississippi.

plank as it was handed to them by the second crew of engineers. The first crew would then place one end of the second plank on the lip of the opposite side of the trench and would set the other end atop the edge of one of the perpendicular two-by-sixes on the first plank. The result was a y-shaped foot bridge the infantrymen were supposed to run down, then up to the other side of the ditch, placing them at the foot of the enemy's earthworks. As it turned out, the bridges didn't work.

I need to pause here and report an anecdote, supposedly true, or every bit as true as everything else I'm writing, due to the fact that I heard it once, about safety precautions on the movie set.

Warner Brothers had not used re-enactors in a war movie before and, accustomed to utilizing whatever passes for normal among movie extras, they had anticipated a lot of injuries. The story circulated through the camps that representatives of the moviemakers came to Natchez before filming commenced, met with the county sheriff, and toured the film site, during which they told him they anticipated 300 to 400 injuries and two to four deaths during the filming.

The latter part of that report may be apocryphal, but the first part was undeniable. They expected a lot of injuries and were prepared for them. Whereas Civil War re-enactors exercise a lot of safety precautions during re-enactments—not carrying ramrods into battle, never running with fixed bayonets, and so forth—Warner Brothers encouraged insane risk for the sake of authenticity. We were expected to act like Civil War soldiers in battle, running full tilt with fixed bayonets, scrambling up steep earthworks with the same, firing point blank at each other, rushing headlong toward firing artillery pieces, and so forth. After each round of filming, the first thing we heard was a loudspeaker announcement, something to the effect of "If you are injured, hold up your hand. If you are near an injured person who is unable to hold up his hand, please hold up yours so medics can find him." Then the wounded would walk or be carried to an ambulance, and filming would resume.

Supposedly there were fewer than 200 injuries during the filming and no deaths, to the great satisfaction of Warner Brothers. Most of the injuries were fairly minor—abrasions and broken bones—although I did observe an incident that caused a man to lose an eye. We were standing around between scenes when a rifle went off nearby and a hat went flying fifteen or twenty feet into the air. I thought it was just a prank, but it turned out that a re-enactor had dropped the butt of his loaded rifle onto the ground, and it had discharged into his face, destroying an eye and sending his hat airborne.

My injury was much less dramatic.

Before filming the assault on the Confederate works, we did three or four walk-throughs and dry runs. We approached the trench, practiced throwing the planks down, secured the two sets into a bridge, and allowed infantrymen to walk across. The engineers' role was relatively straightforward, but we discovered that the foot bridges were springy and unstable and when ran upon were as apt to catapult a man across the trench, or into it, as get him across safely. Warner Brothers' solution was to tell us, the engineers, to stand beside and beneath the bridges and hold them securely with our hands.

Right! When we finally did the filming, with artillery booming, smudge pots exploding to simulate shell explosions, men running and yelling, musketry rolling, powder smoke roiling, and bridges bouncing, the added potential of having a grown man who wasn't an enemy step on your hand, club you with the butt of his rifle, or fall out of the sky and crush you added a certain element of anticipation most Civil War veterans were denied.

Charlie and I had a plank that was one of the front sets, so that we descended into the trench to connect the two ends and, after the first walk-through, we were told to return to our original mark and do it again. We tossed the second plank out of the trench and back to its team of carriers, and everyone in my crew except me walked up our plank and out of the hole. I remained behind to help hoist our plank up and out, which meant I was left stranded at the bottom.

One of my crew leaned down to offer his hand to boost me out. I could not reach it by stretching, so I took a run and jumped to grab it. Our hands connected briefly, I began to fall back and he latched on, catching me by nothing except the end of the ring finger of my right hand. When my full weight connected, the finger snapped at the first joint.

Now I had a dilemma. It was still morning, and if I left to have the finger tended to at the hospital in Natchez, I would be knocked out of the rest of the battle and out of that portion of the movie. I decided to wrap a handkerchief around it and the middle finger and remain on the set, which I did, thinking optimistically that the bandaged hand would make me easier to spot when the show finally débuted.

During the day's filming, as we were running across the battlefield carrying our plank, Charlie stepped into a smudge pot just as it exploded, knocking him down and leaving him covered with white powder and pieces of cork. Inside the moat, both of us were stepped on and nearly brained by the infantryman who dashed across the bridge as we tried to make secure from below. Still, we were in show business.

Finally, when the filming stopped for the day and the customary call for the injured was made, I raised my bandaged hand and was escorted to an ambulance, which was more like a limousine, and, in the company of another injured man, was taken to the hospital.

And all of the foregoing was merely for the purpose of setting the stage for the story that gives this chapter its title.

My traveling companion for the half-hour ride to the clinic was a man in his mid-thirties who was also from Waco, Texas, and who was portraying a Federal cavalry captain. I'll call him "Dave" for the purposes of this yarn. I don't recall the nature of his injury, but it was no more serious than mine and certainly did not interfere with his ability to spin a tale. We discovered mutual interests quickly, and what he told me, by my standards, was remarkable. I don't know if it is true, and I may not get all of the facts right after twenty years, but I'll convey the essence of it.

Dave told me that after graduating from college he joined a Christian ministry or missionary group and went to Canada for a summer to conduct religious revivals in isolated rural communities, particularly those inhabited by Native Americans.

Many of the people he and his group visited and preached to lived in primitive conditions, with no electricity, plumbing, or modern appliances. Among the Indians, he said, the goal was to connect with, or convert, one or more of the elders of the tribe. Once that happened, the rest of the band would usually follow suit, but none of the younger people would break ranks and be won over by the preachers unless doing so was clearly sanctioned by one or more older, respected leader.

On one occasion, Dave said, they held a week-long revival in a community of Sioux or Lakota Indians, and midway through what must have been a lot of old-fashioned Bible-thumping and praise-being, an ancient member of the tribe heard something he liked and came down to the front of the tent to be saved.

That prompted several others to follow suit, and Dave reported that his group of missionaries, of which he was apparently a key speaker, regarded that week's work as some of their best of the summer.

At the end of the week, before they moved on, they received an invitation to have dinner with the old man at his home, which they knew was a particular honor. They accepted, of course, and found that the elderly gentleman lived in a two-room shack constructed of a wide variety of building materials, including plywood, corrugated tin, mismatched pieces of lumber, native stone, and essentially whatever was cast off and available for such use.

They ate a meal which was rather mysterious in content, with no illumination other than the fire in the hearth, and at its conclusion the old man announced that he had a gift to give my future fellow traveler.

A younger member of the man's family was dispatched to the other room of the hut and returned with a battered cardboard box that the old man presented to the missionaries. Inside was a pair of old, beaded, fringed, leather gloves, or gauntlets. The old man made a short speech in broken English about the importance of the religious work the group was doing and said he had owned the gloves since he was a boy, having acquired them after "the battle."

Naturally, putting two and two together, the temptation was to think that maybe, just maybe, "the battle" was the Little Big Horn.

Dave said that it was impossible to be confident of the old man's age and that he could have been anywhere from eighty to well over a hundred. I don't recall if I asked Dave what year his missionary work took place but, comparing his age and mine, it must have been in the mid-to-late 1960s. Thus, if the old man was say, ten, in 1876, he would have been about a hundred years old when he presented the gloves to Dave. It could have happened.

Once Dave returned to Waco, he and his friends examined the pair of gloves carefully in the hope of figuring out some of their provenance. He located and showed them to a man familiar with such items and was told that they were consistent in style and constituency with gloves made by Plains Indians in the last half of the nineteenth century. He also noticed that the little finger of one of the gloves was stretched or worn in a manner that indicated its original owner sported a pinkie ring.

Inquiring of another scholar, he was told that if the gloves were worn by a soldier during the Indian Wars time period, it would have probably been by an officer. This expert also pointed out that West Point graduation rings of the mid to late nineteenth century were worn on the pinkie finger. Finally, he directed Dave's attention to something he had not noticed; that there was some sort of dark substance, or stain, on one of the gloves beneath the bead work.

Dave found a laboratory capable of sampling and testing the substance. It proved to be human blood. He also hit the books and found photos of more than one of the Federal army officers, including George Custer, wearing West Point pinkie rings. More importantly, he found a reference to a gift that Libbie Custer, the general's wife, gave her husband on his twenty-eighth birthday—a pair of beaded Indian gauntlets. Dave counted the number of individual fringes on the sleeves of the gloves. There were twenty-eight on each.

Beside himself with excitement, Dave decided to contact the ultimate repository of historic American artifacts—the Smithsonian Institution. Somebody there agreed to examine the gloves and render an opinion, so he had them delivered and anxiously awaited the result. It took several weeks but finally word arrived with the return of the gauntlets.

The Smithsonian did not detract or dispute any of the information Dave had compiled but reported that there was absolutely no way to corroborate his hopeful theories and that the Institute could not offer any information that might support a conclusion that the gloves belonged to and were worn by George Custer when he was killed at the Little Big Horn on June 25, 1876. The Smithsonian added as a postscript, however, that if Dave desired to donate them to the Institute, they would be accepted.

Dave said the gauntlets were in a safe deposit box in a bank in Waco and were his most prized possession. I, Smithsonian-like, offered to take them off his hands, or at least view them, and he agreed to the latter the next time I was in Waco. Subsequently I lost his contact information and have never made an effort to recover it, so I've never seen the gloves and cannot swear that they exist.

As for his tale, a person wanting to look into it would, it seems, start with Dave's assertion that he found a reference to Libbie Custer giving her husband a set of beaded Indian gauntlets on his twenty-eighth birthday. Following that reasoning, I e-mailed a Custer scholar, author, and artifact collector who responded that Libbie and George were probably in Monroe, Ohio, on his twenty-eighth birthday, in 1867, which didn't rule out the possibility that she would have given him the gloves but suggested otherwise. If the record of her gift was well known, this gentleman should have known of it, but Smithsonian-like, he offered to examine the gloves or a photo of them if I could produce either.

Perhaps Dave really did his research, or perhaps he enjoyed spinning a yarn and watching the expressions on the faces of gullible fellow re-enactors.

As for *North/South II*, when it finally was shown it had no greater or more expectant fans than Charlie Sullivan and me. He left a telephone voice-mail message from Perkiston just before the first episode aired, saying that he was "awash in Miller Light and love for my fellow man," and we anxiously perused each battle scene looking for ourselves and the accompanying glory.

Au contraire. We showed up, but there was no waving of battle flags, no flaunting of bandaged hands, no risking of life and limb to get Yankee soldiers safely across Confederate trenches. Charlie appeared twice, first firing a cannon at First Manassas and then running with a bridge plank at Petersburg. I appeared ever so briefly, over the shoulder of Hal Holbrook as Abe Lincoln, standing in the background occupying a quarter of an inch on the television screen for nearly two seconds.

Such are the vagaries of a motion picture career.

2

Chasing Bonnie, Clyde, and W. D.

Our interest's on the dangerous edge of things,
the honest thief, the tender murderer.

ROBERT BROWNING

"Bishop Blougram's Apology" (1855)

THE MOVIE *BONNIE AND CLYDE*, WITH WARREN BEATTY AND FAYE Dunaway, was released when I was a senior in high school, and it resonated loudly with my best friend, Bill Enfield, and me. We saw it three or four times apiece. After we graduated we took a private senior trip to New Orleans that August, before beginning college the next month, and we made a point of going through Arcadia, Louisiana, to see the spot where the outlaw pair were killed, between that city and Gibsland.

Perhaps today there are signs, souvenirs, and brochures for tourists—at least a rock monument has been erected—but in 1968 there was nothing to direct anyone to the site where Frank Hamer and five other lawmen gunned the couple down in 1934. So, after driving around town a little, Bill and I pulled my 1963 Bellaire into a service station and asked the young man who worked there if he could tell us how to find the spot where Bonnie and

Clyde were killed. He said he didn't know where it was but that we should talk to a middle-aged gentleman who also worked there, saying, "He can tell you. He was there."

That piqued our interest, and as soon as the man finished talking to a customer we approached him and asked where the site of the killings was located. He sort of shook his head and told us that he could tell us, but that there was nothing to see. In fact, he said, unless we knew precisely where it was already, we would not be able to find it, as it was just a spot beside a two-lane Louisiana highway, with no marker and no distinctive features.

"But I'll tell you about it," he said. "I was the one who drove the truck out and towed them and their car back into town."

Whoa!

So he proceeded to tell us a tale I imagine he repeated several hundred times over the years. It was seamless, to the point, and didn't take long to share. It went something like this:

I was just a kid, just out of high school and working right here back in 1934, and the man who owned this place got a call to send a truck out to tow a car in. He told me to go do it, and I don't remember whether he knew to tell me what to expect, but as soon as I got close I knew it wasn't just a normal job.

There were cars parked everywhere, and people all over the place. The car that Bonnie and Clyde were in was alongside the road, all shot up, and people were walking around, looking in it, and trying to get souvenirs. People had stolen some of the lug nuts, people were trying to dig bullets out of trees with their pocket knives, some of Bonnie's hair had been snipped off, and one guy even tried to cut off one of Clyde's fingers to get a ring, but other folks wouldn't let him do it.

They were both still in the car, in the front seat, shot all up. There were some law officers there too, and we got that car hooked up to my tow truck so I could pull it back into town. They just left the bodies in the car, and so as I was driving in to town, when I came to a school, I would stop and let the kids come out, step up on the running boards and look in, so that they could see that crime doesn't pay.

After I got them into town and out of the car, I towed it back here to this station and we worked on it, got it running again, and I drove it around town some. Then the lady they'd stole it from came and claimed it.

That was it, about 300 words to sum up what was probably the highlight of the man's life, at least as to his role in American history. I think we asked him a few more questions but learned only that he had been working at the same filling station in Arcadia, Louisiana, ever since, perhaps with time out to serve in World War II. It had been thirty-four years since Bonnie and Clyde were killed when he told us the tale, which may or may not have been true. He was in his mid-fifties telling a couple of about-to-be college kids what he did when he was our age, and now, a little past his age, I'm passing it a little further down the line, keeping the connection open.

My fascination with Clyde Barrow and Bonnie Parker didn't end that day. I read some books about them, looked at the numerous photographs they took of each other, that were a significant source of their fame, and visited their graves in Dallas. The year I began law school at the University of Houston, 1973, I read an article in a magazine about gangsters and outlaws of the 1920s and 1930s, in which a handful who were still living were interviewed. One of them was William Daniel, or William Deacon, "W. D." Jones.

In the movie, Michael J. Pollard portrays a character named C.W. Moss who rode and ran with the outlaw pair right up to the day they died. It was Moss's cinematic father, in fact, who betrayed the couple to the law and helped arrange their ambush and demise. Actually, Bonnie and Clyde had several running buddies of various calibers, such as the Hamilton brothers, Raymond and Floyd, and Henry Methvin, but the man C.W. most resembled in criminal career was W. D. Jones, at least up to a few months before they were killed.

Jones grew up in the same part of West Dallas from which Clyde and his brothers, as well as Bonnie, hailed. He was a part of their little gang for about a year, during the wildest and most famous parts of their short career, participating in the two major shootouts depicted in the movie—in Joplin and Platte City, Missouri—as well as their near escape in Dexfield Park, Iowa, where Buck Barrow was mortally wounded and his wife, Blanche, was captured. Jones was also present at major events in the outlaws' career that were not depicted in the movie, such as the car wreck that nearly killed Bonnie and the gun battle near Fort Smith, Arkansas, in which Marshal H. D. Humphrey was killed. Along the way he was wounded seven times.

Following the gunfight in Dexter Park on July 24, 1933, however, W. D. decided he had had enough. He left the gang near Clarksville, Mississippi, the first week in September, "after they was healed up enough to get by without me." On November 16, he was betrayed by a young friend and arrested in Houston.

He was tried for his role in the killing of Deputy Sheriff Malcolm Davis in Dallas on January 6, 1933, and was sentenced to fifteen years. In a subsequent trial he had two more years tacked onto his sentence as punishment for "harboring" Bonnie and Clyde. He was released from prison in 1943, tried to join the army to fight in the war but could not pass the physical exam due to his old wounds. He settled in Houston.

In January 1934, Bonnie and Clyde helped engineer a daring prison break, freeing Ray Hamilton and four other prisoners from the Eastham State Prison Farm in Houston County, Texas, killing one lawman and wounding another. One of the men who escaped and joined the little gang was Henry Methvin, and it was Methvin's father, Ivan, who was largely responsible for conspiring with Frank Hamer and getting Bonnie and Clyde killed the following May. In other words, C.W. Moss was a cinematic composite of W. D. Jones and Henry Methvin.

I had never spent any time in Houston before I started law school in September 1973. Why or when I happened to see the magazine interview of Jones, I do not recall, but whenever it was, I particularly noticed the photo of Jones and, in the background, the place where he worked, which was his brother's automotive repair shop right there in the city. I decided, what the hell, I'd give old W. D. a phone call and see if he would talk to me.

The magazine's considerate depiction of Jones's place of employment made it simple, probably to his great chagrin, to find the business and its phone number. I called and asked for W. D. Jones. "Who's this?" was the reply. I gave him my name and was told there was nobody named W. D. Jones employed there.

I suspected that wasn't true, waited an hour, and called again. This time I asked for William Deacon Jones. The man who answered told me that

Jones wasn't there just then and to call back later. I waited another hour and telephoned again. This time the man who answered, different from either who had answered before, told me that W. D. Jones was deceased, having passed away a few months earlier. I asked where he was buried and was given the name of a large cemetery in the city.

I called the cemetery and asked if a W. D., William D., or William Deacon Jones was buried there. The person in the cemetery's office checked the records and told me that no one by that name had ever been interred there. Figuring I had chased W. D. enough, and that he was pretty fed up with being chased, I decided to let the matter go.

That very month, however, I happened to read in the Houston newspaper that W. D. Jones, former running buddy of Clyde Barrow and Bonnie Parker, had been arrested for illegal possession of narcotics. "W. D.," I said to myself, "think about what you're doing. You've been pretty lucky so far."

Forty years: some things change and some things stay the same. At left is William Daniel "W. D." Jones in a mug shot after his arrest in 1933, following his career with outlaws Bonnie Parker and Clyde Barrow. At right is Jones in a mug shot after his arrest in 1973 for possession of narcotics. Photos in the public domain—originally in records of Harris and Dallas Counties, Texas.

Almost a year went by before another newspaper story about Jones caught my eye. Considering that I was usually too covered up with law school assignments to pay attention to local news and considering that I was not trying to keep tabs on the old outlaw, it seems serendipitous that I saw the story. In any event, the report was that Jones had parked his car along a Houston street in such a way that it partially blocked a driveway, whose owner told him to move it and, when Jones refused, the owner went inside his house, retrieved a shotgun, and blew Jones away. A version I read later, which included a photograph of the site of his killing, reported that Jones was escorting a lady to her home, on August 20, 1974, and when he approached the house at 10616 Woody Lane, a jealous boyfriend shot him with a 12-gauge. Still another version stated that he was killed in a drug transaction that went wrong. The photo of the house showed a modest home, the driveway to which could not be distinguished from its yard. There did not appear to be any place to park a car that would seriously block access to the house or street. Poor W. D. He lived near the gun, died near the gun, and then had to explain it to Clyde.

As for the alleged truck driver in Arcadia, a book about the outlaw pair reported the following about the immediate aftermath of their being killed:

> The weapons were placed in Sheriff Jordan's [one of the shooters] car while he and Oakley [another of the six lawmen] drove to Arcadia to fetch the coroner. It was decided to leave the bodies in situ until he arrived so Alcorn and Gault [two other lawmen] were left to guard the car as sightseers were arriving. Meanwhile, Hinton and Hamer [the remaining two lawmen] drove to Gibsland to get a breakdown truck. . . . By the time the lawmen returned, a great crowd had already gathered. "I saw women and kids struggling along with grown men to peek inside to get a better view of the bodies in death in the car," Hinton wrote later. "People were on their hands and knees gathering up the spent shells and digging with pocket knives to retrieve bullets embedded in trees." The coroner, Dr. J. L. Wade, attested that Bonnie and Clyde had died of gunshot wounds at 9:15 A.M., whereupon the wrecker pulled the Ford out of the ditch and hitched it up for the 15 mile journey to Arcadia. Sheriff Jordan and his deputy led the

procession followed by Frank Hamer, and Manny Gault. Ted Hinton
and Bob Alcorn brought up the rear.[1]

Although the reference to fetching a breakdown truck (i.e., a truck for
cars that had broken down) from Gibsland, rather than Arcadia, doesn't fit,
the rest of the story seems consistent. Perhaps Hinton and Hamer found no
truck available in Gibsland and so called for one in Arcadia.

There is no mention in the article of stopping at schools along the route
to town. But an Internet site yielded the following as the caption to a photo
of an old school in Gibsland:

> After the ambush, Bonnie and Clyde, shot to pieces and all gory, were
> towed inside their stolen car to the coroner's office in Arcadia. The
> way to Arcadia is through the little town of Gibsland. Right in front of
> the town school, the tow truck with its gruesome cargo broke down.
> Above is that old Gibsland school, where the kids spilled out of the
> doors to get a firsthand look inside the "death car" (a lesson that crime
> doesn't pay?)[2]

Maybe the truck didn't stop but broke down. Maybe it simply stopped
rather than broke down. Maybe thirty-four years eroded some of the gentleman's memory. I know that the forty years since Bill and I paused in
Arcadia for an hour has seriously eroded mine, but then if I was certain of
what is correct and what is not, these stories might be considered true history instead of trash history.

3

Jackson and Janie

Golden lads and girls all must, as chimney
sweepers, come to dust.
SHAKESPEARE
Cymbeline, Act IV

ANYONE WHO ENJOYED, OR ENDURED, THE 2003 MOVIE *GODS AND
Generals* may recall scenes near the end depicting the brief, poignant relationship between Lieutenant General Thomas J. "Stonewall" Jackson and
five-year-old Jane Corbin.

The movie was faithful to history in a heavy-footed, plodding manner
and was of a rare type that many devoted Civil War enthusiasts craved,
while other, allegedly normal people responded to it with thoughts of vein-
opening and self-immolation. For those who did not see the movie or who
have blocked it from memory, the story goes like this:

Jane Wellford Corbin was the only daughter of a couple named Richard
and Roberta Corbin who lived on a large plantation near Fredericksburg,
Virginia, called Moss Neck. Richard served in the Confederate army, and
the family owned another home in Fredericksburg called Corbin Hall, but
the mansion at Moss Neck was sometimes called by that name as well.

Following the battle of Fredericksburg, which was a significant Confederate victory fought on December 13, 1862, General Lee moved his army into winter quarters in areas surrounding the city, and his Second Corps, which was commanded by Jackson, occupied land owned by the Corbins. Jackson was invited to make his headquarters at Moss Neck, and while he characteristically declined to occupy a private home for military purposes, Mrs. Corbin was able to convince him to move into a small building located behind the house that was used as an office. He and his wing of Lee's army remained there until the following spring.

Jackson, up to then, had not had the best of luck with wives or children. His first wife, Eleanor Junkin, died in childbirth with the child, and his second wife, Anna Morrison, miscarried a child early in the war. She had, however, given birth to another child, a daughter named Julia, mere weeks before. Mother and child were living with family at Cottage Home, in North Carolina, and Jackson had not seen his baby daughter yet. Letters and concern for their welfare occupied much of the general's thoughts and time not devoted to military or spiritual matters. So it was that when young Janie Corbin began coming to Jackson's headquarters, seemingly as fond of the old warrior as he was of children, a heartwarming relationship developed.

Jackson was not famous for being either loving or lovable. A military genius, he was also an extremely strict taskmaster and disciplinarian who showed no mercy to either the enemy or any of his own soldiers who failed to do their duty. Add to that an extreme, fundamental Christian belief system, plus some decidedly odd views on health care and the workings of his own body, and the product was startling if not totally off-putting to many of his peers. He was rarely known to display a sense of humor, although the joyful young cavalry commander, J.E.B. Stuart, was able to coax or prod an occasional grin out of him. He was extremely modest and incapable of taking credit or for that matter giving credit to hardly anyone except his Presbyterian God. Most importantly, he won battles, and, in teamwork with Robert E. Lee, he was practically unstoppable. Had he not been mortally wounded by his own men the following May, in the Battle of Chancellorsville, it is conceivable that the South would have been successful at Gettysburg and might even have won the Civil War.

Those few months, from mid-December to March, were an idyllic time

Moss Neck plantation house, depicted in the 1912 issue of *Confederate Veteran* magazine that contained an article by Jane Corbin's mother about what occurred there in 1862–1863. Courtesy of *Confederate Veteran*, January 1912.

for the Confederacy and for Jackson. The disasters and heartaches that would dominate mid-1863 and the hard-driving ruthlessness of U.S. Grant and William Sherman that would follow in 1864 were unknown and unknowable. General Lee and his staff celebrated Christmas in the Moss Neck mansion, and romance blossomed between Jackson's chief of staff, Sandy Pendleton, and Mrs. Corbin's sister-in-law, Kate Corbin. For more than three months the war was essentially held in limbo. As far as anyone in or near Jackson's headquarters at Moss Neck knew, their future would be as bright and shining as their present.

Janie was a delight. Jackson's staff officer, Henry Kyd Douglas, described her as having a "wealth of light golden hair . . . large trustful, wistful eyes, 'sweetest eyes were ever seen,' and . . . perfect unspoiled ways."[3] She would visit the general every day, and when he wasn't engaged in military affairs, he would carry on conversations with the little girl or attempt to teach her various matters of educational value. When he was working, she would content herself cutting out paper dolls in the shape of little soldiers, which she called her "Stonewall Brigade." It was not unusual, although quite eye-opening, to see "Old Blue Light" giving her rides on his shoulders or walking hand in hand with her around the estate. This wasn't the taciturn, Old Testament warrior his soldiers were accustomed to, and the relationship did not go unnoticed.

Janie probably knew that Jackson was a great hero but could not have comprehended the rock-star status he had achieved in the Southern Confederacy. Had the subject of his popularity or reputation for success come up, Jackson almost certainly would have blushed, declined any personal credit, and changed the subject. He just wanted to do his duty, serve his Lord, and let God's will be done. More than anything, he wanted to see his wife and baby daughter, and Janie's company must have been his most cherished substitute for them.

Douglas witnessed the event around which this little tale evolves, writing of it in his war memoirs, *I Rode with Stonewall:*

> I went over to Corbin Hall to see her [Janie] one day and found her standing between the General's knees and they had been having some conversation on the subject of writing, for he was showing her some paper that had been written on and she was listening very attentively. Her rich curling hair would fall over her face and she would throw it back with graceful gestures as she tried to look up at him. He asked her what had become of her comb which kept it back and she said it was broken. With a smile, as if a pleasing thought had occurred to him, he picked up the brilliant cap of which I have spoken at Fredericksburg, looked at it and at her head for a moment and then proceeded to cut off the gilt band which encircled the cap. Having done this, he picked out the threads and then bound this golden band around her golden hair and, holding up her face in his hands, he asked her to wear that for him. Her face lighted up like a sunbeam and with a cry of delight she ran off to show it to her mother.[4]

The cap, a billed forage cap, sometimes called a bummer or, inaccurately for this style of headgear, a kepi, had accompanied a gift of a stylish, handsome uniform bestowed on the general by J.E.B. Stuart just before the battle of Fredericksburg. Stuart was renowned for flair, fashion, and dash, whereas Jackson was notoriously unkempt and threadbare. Jackson at first refused to wear the uniform but finally consented, and the sight of his new splendor became the talk of the army, perhaps all of the Confederacy. The unexpected manifestation was topped off by a new forage cap, given him by one of Stuart's staff officers, the Prussian Heros Von Borke, who was quite a bon vivant in his own right.

Jane Welford Corbin, or "Janie." This may be the only existing portrait of the little girl who first stole, then broke, the heart of Confederate General Thomas Jonathan "Stonewall" Jackson. Courtesy of *Confederate Veteran*, January 1912.

Sadly, the happy times of Jackson and Janie came to a tragic end. In March the Second Corps broke camp and moved off toward the spring campaign, and almost simultaneously Jane Corbin came down with what proved to be scarlet fever. She, along with two young cousins, did not recover from the disease.

When Jackson received the news of his little friend's death he was utterly and totally heartbroken. This fierce warrior who had seen hundreds of men and close associates slain in battle or felled by disease, this unyielding combatant whose remedy for dealing with brave foemen was to "kill them all," hung his head and wept openly and freely as his officers and staff looked on, utterly powerless to do or say anything appropriate.

The general's wife and daughter, Julia, joined him at his camp on April 20 for the father's first visit with daughter. On May 2, Jackson was mortally wounded, and he died on May 10, with wife and daughter in attendance during his last few lingering days.

This story struck a chord with me, being a nice little package of history, hero worship, and poignancy, and I wondered what became of the golden band. The only reference I found was a passage in a biography of Mrs. Jackson titled *The Gallant Mrs. Stonewall*. It mentioned that "to prevent contagion, the clothes of the Moss Neck children were burned."

This did not specifically say that the golden cap band was burned, but it was certainly inferred. Why else would the act of burning the clothes even be mentioned?

A few years before the movie, I read the story again and, inspired and a little heartbroken, I wrote a poem—song lyrics actually—about the incident, as follows.

JACKSON AND JANIE

The winter between the victories, the second of the war,
when Jackson lived behind her house those months that numbered four,
Janie Corbin, five years old, of the place called Corbin's Hall,
did what Lincoln's men could not, and captured Old Stonewall.

No cannonade nor mass assault, no drum or marching tune
were used in her offensive as she came each afternoon
armed with trusting eye, wealth of curl and unspoiled smile.
Her strategy much more than matched the warrior's genius guile.

Chorus: And he thought of his own Julia, then a babe at Cottage Home,
and his heart longed for some happiness in a world he would never own,
for between his Julia and five years old was a place called Chancellorsville
and a hole in the heart of all the South that time would never heal.

One day as he taught Janie lessons of the power of pen or prayer,
she listened, gazing into his eyes, and she brushed away her hair.
"Where's your comb?" Old Stonewall asked. "'Tis broken," was her reply,
and the old blue light he was famous for came sparkling to his eye.

He took his fine new forage cap, the one with the golden band,
the one he'd worn at Fredericksburg when he'd never looked so grand.
He'd worn it with the new gray uniform JEB Stuart had endowed,
as he stole another victory from Burnside's Yankee crowd.
                              (Chorus)
Just a few snips of his sharpened blade removed the golden lace.
He picked out the threads and held it up before sweet Janie's face.

Then binding the gold in the girl's blond hair, he smiled at her tenderly.
"Those curls will stay in place," he said, "if you'll wear this just for me."

Sweet Janie squealed with child's delight and with firmest sincerity,
swore she'd wear it all her days, which sadly came to be,
for scarlet fever on cat's paws crept when Spring was four weeks old
and stole from Janie Corbin her unspoiled five year soul.
(Chorus)
When Jackson heard the tragic news that little Jane had died,
the mighty warrior trembled, and hanged his head and cried.
Joys are stolen from some men's lives while some find a few to keep.
Little Janie was the very last to make Old Stonewall weep.

Like all her things, that golden band was delivered to cleansing flame
as was the custom when the fever claimed another name.
Of all the lost treasures in this world, a Southern heart understands
that very few can shine as bright as that simple golden band.

The Oregon musician Bill Coleman put the lyrics to music, included them on a CD of other Civil War songs titled *The Last Roses,* and incorporated the song into one of the Civil War musical dramas that he and his wife, Carla, perform throughout the country. Bill's music and rendition of the song are so well done, so powerful, that I have seen grown men break into tears and sobs at its conclusion.

One day on their travels, a fan of the Colemans told them of an article he or she had read in an old issue of the *Confederate Veteran.* The magazine, published from 1893 to 1932, was about and often written by veterans of the Confederate army about subjects of interest to them and their families. It provides a wealth of historic information, and the particular article the fan was talking about, published in the January 1912 issue, was written by none other than Mrs. Roberta Gary Corbin Kinsolving, the mother of Janie.

Her husband was killed in the war, but she later remarried, and the story was published nearly fifty years after the events it described occurred. She wrote of the incidents leading up to the battle, the excitement of the combat, and, on December 16, 1862, the arrival of Stonewall Jackson at her home. Of Jackson and Janie she wrote:

General Jackson was not only a great soldier but a man as loving and as tender as a woman in his sympathies and interests. "The bravest are the tenderest, the loving the most daring." He was very fond of children, especially little Jane Wellford Corbin, our only child, who was at this time about five years of age, winning in her ways, and the pet and darling of the whole staff. Indeed, she was beloved by all our army friends. General Jackson would send for her to come to the office and see him in the mornings. She would play there for hours at a time. She would sit on the floor, cut paper dolls, and entertain the General with her childish prattle.

One favorite amusement of his as well as hers was the folding of a piece of paper and cutting a long string of dolls all joined together in ranks which she called her "Stonewall Brigade." I can imagine a smile and a merry twinkle in his eyes as he scanned these miniature soldiers, funny little bow-legged fellows they were. I have some of them now between the leaves of my old Bible. I am sure any of the old veterans would laugh to see their diminutive representation.

Janie particularly admired the new military cap with its broad gilt band, not long before sent to the General by Mrs. Jackson [Note—Mrs. Jackson did give her husband a forage cap that he wore through the Valley Campaign and until the invasion of Maryland prior to the Battle of Sharpsburg, but the cap of which Mrs. Kinsolving wrote was a later gift and not from Mrs. Jackson], and she also admired the new uniform which I have heard was given to him by Gen. J.E.B. Stuart, which was worn the day of the battle of Fredericksburg, making him thus unconsciously a target for the enemy.

One day he took the end of his pen knife, and, ripping the band from the cap, he pinned it round the child's hair like a coronet, he said "Janie, it suits a little girl like you better than it does an old soldier like me." She came running in, her eyes sparkling, to show it to mother and to tell what he said. Afterwards, she wore it in the same ornamental way when she was dressed for the evening. Regally she wore her crown; the gold of the band blended with the gold in her hair. Dear little girl, we did not dream that for this gift of General Jackson, her name would become historic. The incident has been mentioned in many a history as an evidence of his great loving heart and regard for little children. The little piece of braid, now faded and tarnished, I kept and am preserving still as a precious souvenir with priceless associations.

Not many weeks afterwards, this lovely child was seized with malignant scarlet fever, and in less than forty-eight hours this dreadful scourge of childhood had ended her sweet young life. She died the very morning after General Jackson left Moss Creek to prepare to open his spring campaign. She seemed but the avant courier of the brilliant star so soon to set. Only a month or two later Jackson too was taken away from us.

She still had the golden band in 1912? It wasn't burned? Of all the lost treasures in this world, this one a southern heart understands that very few can shine as bright as . . . isn't lost after all? Where the #@%! is it?

Her name was Kinsolving in 1912. That couldn't be too common a name. Carla Coleman and I went on the hunt. She and Bill visited Moss Neck, which is still standing and in private ownership, although they were not allowed to walk the grounds, look for Janie's grave, or peer inside the office. Before long, she and I both made progress closing in on the braid.

I was able to make contact with Charles "Les" Kinsolving, of Vienna, Virginia, whose name might be familiar because he is a White House correspondent. Despite his lofty elevation in world events, he graciously corresponded with me by mail and on the phone. He recalled the story, acknowledged being related to Janie's mother's second husband, and remembered that the braid passed into the ownership of a rather eccentric or colorful uncle, who was bit of a rascal. He said he believed the uncle had ultimately turned it over to the Museum of the Confederacy in Richmond. He had never heard of or about the paper Stonewall Brigade dolls.

Carla, in the meantime, was directed independently toward the Museum of the Confederacy She contacted officials there and was told, yes, it did have a piece of gold braid that was donated to the museum by a Kinsolving relative in the 1920s or 1930s. It was not on display, but a photo was available.

Carla obtained the photo, and we stared at it. Something didn't look right. It appeared to be about the right length to encircle a forage cap, but it was not like the type of gold braid or tape we were accustomed to seeing on Civil War headgear. Still, if that was what all the fuss we'd made was about, we were, well, glad to finally lay eyes on it, seeing as how it was a lost treasure and all. Bill Coleman looked at it, and said he didn't think it came from a cap. Carla and I didn't let him see us roll our eyes. Bill Coleman is a Yankee and couldn't be expected to have appropriate reverence for certain holy relics, even if he did sing a song about this one well enough to make people cry.

A few weeks later I had the less-than-brilliant idea that it should be possible to match the braid in the Museum of the Confederacy with the forage cap Old Stonewall snipped it from. I went on the hunt for Stonewall's caps.

One of the General's caps, a round-brimmed blue model from the Virginia Military Institute, where he taught before the war, and which he wore at the Battle of First Manassas, is in the Museum of the Confederacy in Richmond. Another, similar cap, sort of grayish-brown in color, is in the VMI museum and is described in a book as being the one he wore at Fredericksburg. Trouble was, that one still has a band of gold braid encircling it.

This confused me for awhile, but I finally found reference to this latter cap having been in the possession of Major Jed Hotchkiss, Jackson's mapmaker and a staff officer, who wrote that Stonewall wore it through the Valley, Seven Days, and Second Manassas campaigns but that at Frederick

Braid purported to be from Stonewall Jackson's cap that he removed and gave Janie Corbin and that was donated to the Museum of the Confederacy by Reverend Wythe L. Kinsolving in 1934, later determined by the museum to be from a pair of military trousers. Reprinted by permission of Museum of the Confederacy, Richmond, Virginia. Photography by Katherine Wetzel.

City, Maryland, during the Sharpsburg Campaign, Hotchkiss bought the general "a soft hat" and that Jackson then gave Hotchkiss the forage cap when they were at Fredericksburg. There is an engraving of Jackson at the Battle of Sharpsburg wearing a hat with a full brim. The one in the VMI museum is the one given to him by Mrs. Jackson. The cap Jackson wore at Fredericksburg, and from which he snipped the gold braid to give to Janie, was missing in action and, as of this writing, still is. It was found on the battlefield by a Confederate soldier the day after the general's wounding, and the soldier delivered it to General Dorsey Pender, but its fate thereafter is at least cloudy, if not nonexistent.

I contacted some members of the modern Stonewall Brigade, a group of re-enactors. Some are Civil War trekkies and some are scholars, and I attempted to enlist their aid in locating the missing cap. One, Eric Mink, added a new log to my smoldering fire, e-mailing me on May 6, 2008, to report:

> Nothing more on the cap, but there have been some recent developments with the braid TJJ gave to little Janie Corbin. In 1934 a Corbin descendant gave to the Museum of the Confederacy a 1" by 22" strip of gold braid, believed to be a piece from TJJ's cap and the one given to Janie. As it turns out, this piece of braid is actually from either TJJ's coat or from his trousers. The real piece of gold cap braid turned up recently and was sold by a Virginia antiques dealer. The new owner is a private collector, and I had the pleasure of viewing the braid recently. The curator of the MOC [Museum of the Confederacy] agrees that what the museum has is not the cap braid given to Janie, but that that piece of cloth is in the hands of the private collector.

One suspects that the donator to the MOC, whose name was Reverend Wythe L. Kinsolving, was the eccentric uncle remembered by Les Kinsolving. The MOC received the braid in 1934, and perhaps the reverend believed it was the cap braid or believed it was from a uniform owned by Jackson, perhaps not. Perhaps, just perhaps, by telling people it was the Janie Corbin gold braid, he was then free to sell the real braid to a willing, discreet buyer without having to share any of the sales proceeds with the rest of his Depression-era family.

Then in January 2010, while gathering the illustrations for this book, I was able to make indirect contact with the private collector who owns the real Jackson-Janie braid. I never talked to him, dealing strictly through third-party common acquaintances, Eric Mink, and a curator at the Museum of the Confederacy, and while the owner finally agreed to allow the braid to be photographed and published, it was only with the condition that he remain anonymous and that the braid be described in the book only as having a "strong provenance."

I understand that conviction completely. Besides those who might attempt to steal such an artifact if they knew where it was, there are those who believe that noteworthy historic items should not be allowed to be owned privately. I need not comment on what I consider to be the un-American and silly nature of such a belief system, but a man who cares enough about such items to save and protect them does not need to be criticized for doing so any more than does the owner of a painting by Picasso.

On January 15, 2010, just as I was approaching the deadline for finalizing the illustrations, I received the photograph and permission for it to be included in the book. To other people this might be nothing more than an interesting historical footnote. To me it was fulfillment of a dream. The image of that simple golden band is published here for, as far as I know, the first time in history.

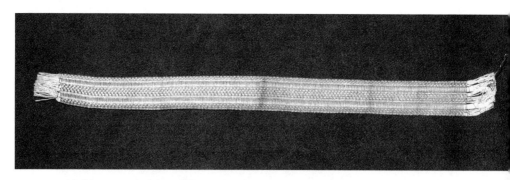

"Of all lost treasures of this world, a Southern heart understands that very few can shine as bright as that simple golden band." Considered lost for decades, made famous in story, song, and cinema, this is the first published photo of the cap braid that Jackson gave to Janie Corbin to tie up her hair a few weeks before she died of scarlet fever and he was mortally wounded in battle. Courtesy of a private collection, with strong provenance. Photograph by Eric Mink.

To someone who cares about such things, no explanation is necessary. For those who do not care but happen to be reading these words anyway, consider that the Civil War was our country's greatest crisis and tragedy and that it completely altered, as well as salvaged, the fabric of our nation, thereby changing and in many ways determining the future of world events. Then consider that following the war, as the nation gradually healed and the war took on mythic status, the story of Jackson, Janie, and the gold braid became not only important to those who were associated with it or who worshipped the memory of Jackson and his men but to thousands of people who loved the story's romance and poignancy. The story faded with the passing of the veterans and others who endured the war, but books mentioned it, a movie depicted it, a song described it, and interest was renewed.

Next, consider that the braid uniquely symbolizes and embodies the Old South and its passing from existence, but whereas *Gone with the Wind* and its ilk are fanciful fiction, the braid is a genuine relic that belonged to one of the most famous characters of the time, given to a young lady who symbolized all contemporary hope for the future—a hope which was tragically short-lived.

Finally, consider that the braid was believed by many to be lost forever, due primarily to words I wrote, so that publication of this photo is, at least to some folks, tantamount to recovery and restoration of a national treasure.

The world turns on. Lives come and go. Hopes, dreams, joys, and tragedies play themselves out on the great stage, where we each hope to make a difference. Certainly I hoped in optimistic youth to be more than a stagehand who reported that a minor prop from a particular production was missing, only to discover I was wrong. Nevertheless, sitting in my rocking chair as the sun sets or reliving memories in my last bed, the story of the Jackson-Janie cap braid will drift near the zenith of my recollections.

4

Old Letters

You bid me burn your letters. But I must forget you first.

LETTER FROM JOHN ADAMS TO ABIGAIL ADAMS

April 28, 1776

★

SOME PEOPLE IN SOME PLACES COLLECT SOME OF NEARLY EVERYTHING. Historical artifacts, especially those associated with heroes, wars, and battles, are particularly popular, and among the most valuable and sought-after of those are the ones that have the greatest association with great events, great people, or great romance.

Near the top of the list of collectible artifacts are weapons, flags, uniforms, belt plates, antique photographs of soldiers, military buttons, and items with unusual or interesting stories to tell. Lower on such lists in order of popularity are several intervening items before one comes to old letters. They are above newspapers but probably not above bullets and certainly not above arrowheads.

There are a variety of reasons why old letters, even from historical times, do not excite people. Unless a letter was signed by somebody famous, it has to be read in order to be appreciated. This is time-consuming.

A tourist cannot simply stroll by a display case, glance at a letter, and admire its significance. He or she has to exert more effort than is popular on a vacation. Additionally, some people's handwriting, poor spelling, and grammar, or the physical condition of the letter makes it tedious or challenging to decipher the significance. Also, of course, the content of most letters is mind-numbingly boring.

For a historical letter that was not written by a famous personage to be an attention-grabber, it not only needs to contain interesting content but pretty much needs the assistance of an interpreter and a publicist. The few discussed hereafter, most of which have come into my possession, will have that assistance. (The first two Virgil Duc letters are held in another private collection.)

The charm of letters, their romance, at least to some collectors, is that they are, or were, so personal to their original writers and recipients. They insert the modern reader into the minds of persons who lived long ago and experienced, firsthand, events and lifestyles we know today only through movies, books, and museums. Some conjure up mental snapshots or virtual-reality emotions. Some will bring on a smile, many will touch the heart, and some will bring a tear to the eye.

An example is a letter written by a young wife, Jane W. Dowell Smith, a.k.a. Jennie, to her husband, John A. Smith, an Ohio state legislator, the day after Valentine's Day in 1843. He was apparently at the state capitol, doing what legislators do, and she was back in Highland, Ohio, keeping the home fires burning and caring for their young child. She was obviously well-educated and articulate, with a quick mind and magnetic personality, the kind of lady any of us might be drawn to at any modern social gathering.

She began the one-page epistle teasingly, to let the man she loved know that he should not assume she was missing him unduly, saying

> "[D]on't let the member from Highland suppose for a moment that
> Mrs. John A. Smith is going to indulge him with a letter of any length.
> By no means. If she cannot be gratified in what little bit of curiosity
> she has, she has no idea of gratifying others, besides any one that could
> be bought up with a kiss can't be trusted with her secrets, though they
> may be as numerous as the sands of the sea shore. . . ."

After continuing in this vein for a few lines, she switched to the favorite topic of all young parents, the things done and said by their child, in this case a son, three or four years of age, named Jimmy. She wrote:

> We have had such delightful sleighing as we have not had before for five years, not since the winter we were married. The streets are full of sleighs, and Jimmy is almost crazy. The bells delight him very much. He says "me does wish me had dem on my neck, me go tingle ringle tingle ringle." He stays at the window continually watching for his papa. He is sure you will come to ride [with] him. He says, "the sleighs has no wheels, dey just got their foots turned up."

The image of that child at the window, the snow-covered scene, the jingling of bells, the horse-drawn sleighs, the lad's cute description, and the longing of mother and child for the man they love pulls as irresistibly at one's heart now as it must have pulled at John A. Smith's 165 years ago.

Other letters are charming because they transport the modern reader to a place, lifestyle, and social mind-set that no longer exists and never will again, particularly with regard to the battle of the sexes. Take for example, a letter written on October 1, 1848, by Charles J. C. Puckett, Jr. to Miss Elvira Yost, who lived at Campti plantation, near Minden, in Natchitoches Parish, Louisiana.

Charles began the message casually, acknowledging the receipt of a letter from her the week before the previous week and explaining that he could not reply more promptly due to being sick with a fever. Then he launched into an explanation, or plea for mercy, about something that had certainly been making him feverish of late, saying:

> Dear friend, you must indeed pardon me for writing the last letter on the subject I did. I was a fool to think, much less hope, that I would be answered, or even noticed by you. I was, at that time, thoughtless of what, how, or to whom I was writing.
>
> Hereafter, if you would condescend to oblige your best friend and well-wisher, you will (if it pleases you) write a friendly letter only and

I will write you as at first. Do, dear friend, write as usual. I know that
I have done wrong by writing to you as I did. Therefore, forgive me if
you have any pity on your friend, Charly.

Obviously, Charly had become too forward with Elvira in his previous
letter, and she had put him back in his place, even slapped and slammed
him down in her reply. We can only imagine what he might have said and
how she must have responded. The temptation is to imagine some cumber-
some, boorish compliments from him and some stilted "what kind of lady
do you take me for" response from her, delivered via a *Gone with the Wind*
mating-dance ritual in which her words shouted, "No!" while her tone said,
"Tell me more and come hither." That she conveyed that subtle message, or
that Charly was so moonstruck that he could not resist believing it existed,
is revealed in the last line on the page.

Following his apologetic plea for future friendship only, he wrote two
more paragraphs of news about the weather, illness in the region, the un-
common lowness of the river, a visit from a mutual friend, and the friend's
plan to return to school. He closed with "Your best friend in existence" and
signed his full name. Then, in the same hand but in ink of another color,
perhaps added later in the day as a postscript, he wrote "Beautiful being
with starlike eyes."

Oh, Charly. . . .

Another small collection of one-sided correspondence that captures the
same awkwardly stilted notions of romance that pervaded the time are contained in three letters written by a young Confederate officer in late 1863
and early 1864 to a woman in Charleston, South Carolina. His name was
Virgil Duc and hers was Antoinette. One must read between the lines and
puzzle a bit to figure out exactly what was going on, but the picture that
finally emerges is simultaneously charming and hideously goofy.

In the first, which is undated, Virgil uses the lady's first name, showing
familiarity, and immediately launches into what was on his mind:

My Dear Antoinette,
    You have told me you loved me and you are already aware of the
deep wealth of affection which my heart contains for you. Everything
I do is for your welfare and happiness in this world and future bliss

above. Therefore I hope and trust you will not take offense at that which I am about to write. Did I not really and truly love you, I would say nothing to you of it.

Antoinette, I ask you to give up the organ, will you do it? If you do then will I be confident that your affection is sincere, but if on the contrary you refuse then I will be certain that you of course do not care for me. I will now explain why I wish you to leave it. Do not think I would ask such a favor, did I not have a very serious cause.

Your name is in the mouth of every one not as I would wish the girl that I love to be spoken about, but on the contrary my feelings have been many times wounded by the careless prattle of a set of loafers. Moreover the Ladies who visit that Choir are not the ones with which I would permit a wife of mine to associate.

Do not judge me too hastily and say I am slandering that I know nothing of them. I am not slandering but I am a man, and of course I hear things of which you, as a Lady, know nothing. Therefore Antoinette, choose now at once and forever between me or the organ, for if you will still return the latter then will I be compelled to leave you until you do give it up. If you do prefer the Choir then for God's sake for your Parents and for your own sake if not for mine associate no more with the Ladies who go in the Choir. Ponder well ere you choose for your fair name will be sullied if you still continue in the company of them. Once more I entreat I implore you by all your hopes of happiness to quit the Choir.

Oh, Antoinette, my dearest one you do not know the wickedness of this world and how soon a young Lady may lose her good name, even though she is innocent. A young Lady is always respected or disrespected according to the company in which she is generally seen. I have now shown you the effects of evil company and I feel assured that your good judgment will not cause you to delay in leaving the choir. Will you do it for the sake of your good name?

While in Fort Sumter I found a piece of Yankee shell—the fuse of which I had a ring made. If you consent to give up the Choir let me see this ring on your finger when I return from Sumter which will be in the space of three weeks. If you do not wear it I will of course know your answer to the request of . . . Virgil

Wait a minute. Give up the organ? Did we read that right? "Choose now at once forever between me or the organ"? Oh, Virgil. . . . And what about that ring made out of a piece of exploded shell fuse? That must have been one ugly piece of jewelry any young lady would be oh-so-proud to display on a finger.

Apparently Antoinette refused to give up the organ, for in the next letter, written after a few weeks had passed, Virgil assumed a whistling-in-the-dark, above-it-all manner and ignored the fact that he previously made a complete and utter ass of himself or, more accurately, that he had thrown his gauntlet to the ground and she had kicked it into the gutter.

He had that very morning, December 1, 1863, apparently after a period of waiting, heard back from her, but he tried to be businesslike in his unromantic but immediate response. He no longer trumpeted his love for her and did not suggest that they would be married someday, reporting only common news in a clipped, disjointed, I'll-show-you-I'm-not-heartbroken manner, while also making certain she would know where he would be just in case she wanted to find him, writing,

Dear Miss Antoinette,

I received your letter this morning I was more than happy to hear from you. I must ask your pardon for heading my last letter with dear Antoinette instead of Miss Antoinette.

I presume you heard that three men from the Charleston Battalion deserted to the yankees on last Friday night. I am going to ask for a furlough in ten days time. I will try and get it so I can have Christmas at home. I am going to get that pass that General Hagood promised me when I was in the city. I will try and get it and be in the city on next Sunday. I made an application to the General to go to Wilmington. The application was returned saying that the Regt was under orders. Lieut. Col. Pressley told me that he would not be surprised if we go West. I hope it is not true. I would not like to go out West without tents. I think it is cold enough on James Island without having to go West without tents. I was on picket on last Sunday in all that rain.

Since I commenced this letter orders have come to our Regt to move to Secessionville. General Hagood told our Col. that the enemy was going to attack Secessionville.

Have you received any music from home? I had my hand burnt five times with caustic. Dr. Ravenel told me that I would not be able to use my hand for a month. Tell Henry I will answer his letter tomorrow. Capt Muzzek & Lieut Duc all report on the sick list. Lieut Lalune is on court martial. Give my love to all. Yours Truly, Virgil Duc

Three and a half months passed before his next letter or at least the next one that has come to light. It is in poor condition compared to the other two, with portions that have dissolved or been eaten away, so that it is only partially legible. What remains nevertheless completes an image, demonstrates that romance was still alive in the heart of Virgil Duc, suggests that Antoinette may even have been wearing his ring, and inserts cloak-and-dagger intrigue into their fragile relationship. It is copied below as it exists, missing parts included:

Camp Perrin,
James Island,
April 16th, 1864

Dear Miss Antoinette,
    Excuse the liberty I assume in addressing you in an epistolary [i.e. in a manner suitable for a letter] form; nor would I assume such a position did I not believe that the intimacy which existed between us as friends and you failing to return my letters entitled me to that privilege. I did not withdraw from my engagement on account of your not leaving the Choir: it was because you read my letters to some young men that is my ——. If you can prove to me that it was —— —— clearly (?) done, we will (if you——) —— the same friendship as of old. —— —— —— write to me during the —— —— —— ——
    Your obedient servant, Virgil Duc
    PS Dear Antoinette, I must —— —— that I do. I think that anything will ever be right.
    PS If you do not feel inclined to write, return your letters and the ring by your Brother. This letter will be handed to you by Maggie McMannis so that no one will be aware of your having received it. Therefore, on it alone seek advice or counsel from no person. Let your

own heart be your dictator. If you desire that we should be the same old of friends return by bearer, if ——Respectfully —— ——in a package so that even she will know nothing of it.

It is possible, highly likely in fact, that the ladies about whom Virgil warned Antoinette so sincerely were prostitutes who were utilizing the cover story of being in a choir to gain access to the soldiers' camps. It is also possible, of course, that Antoinette was one of them, and that Virgil was too naïve and love struck to realize it. We cannot know but that his letters, particularly the first one, were passed hand to hand or read aloud, not only to the young men Virgil heard and wrote about but to every other lady of ill-repute in the choir, some or all of whom rolled on the floor howling with laughter. We can also surmise, or guess, that Virgil was grasping at the fact that she had not returned his letters as a straw-like indicator that she might still give a damn (that's *GWTW* talk).

On the other hand, Antoinette was probably as pure as the snow, as sweet as the organ she fingered, as innocent as Virgil, and perhaps she cared as deeply for him as he did for her. The reference in the last letter to her brother, as well as other mutual acquaintances, makes it likely that Virgil knew her and her family and that she was as chaste and innocent a young lady as Virgil envisioned her to be. Perhaps additional information will come to light someday about the pair.

Other letters capture great tragedy that occurred in people's lives, such as the one written in Baton Rouge by a member of an Illinois regiment to the mother of one of his comrades. Its purpose was to tell her of the death of her son, and it follows with the original spelling and punctuation preserved.

Post Hospital
August 4th, 1863
Baton Rouge, La

Mrs. Clara C. Kulin (or Keelin):
    I tak this opertunity of droping you these few lines to inform you of the death of your son Jesse. he died this morning at five o'clock A.M. I was with him until he died i had a long talk with him the night

before he died his Request was that his remains should be taken home and buried alongside of his father he spoke frequently of his Mother and Sister he said he was prepared to die the last word that could be understood from him was heaven. and then past of without a strugel and closed his eyes to wake no more. Jesse was well thought of by his company and all that mad their acquaintance with him.

You can com or send some one her for his remains you can com to the Post Hospital and get his effects and they will direct you to the resting place of his body he is buried this morning with Military honer. I will send you some of his hair in this letter. I believe there is no more information that I can give you.

I Remain very Respectfully yours,

Louis L. Burns[5]

Member of Co. D, 11th Ills. Inf.

Sometimes a letter will capture a mystery but leave it unsolved, as does one dated April 15, 1864, written by a Confederate soldier named William J. Woodley, stationed in Tallahassee, Florida, to a friend in Woodley's native state of North Carolina. After a couple of obligatory opening remarks, he wrote:

Warren, please write me on the receipt of this and let me know every-thing concerning my sister Mary. Keep nothing from me if you please. I don't think it will ever answer for me to return to North Carolina again. Warren, since what I have heard about Mary, my heart is nearly broken. Though no one knows everything of it here, yet it hurts me day and night. I think it will not be long before I go to my grave and when I go, I shall go with a bleeding heart. May God forgive me, but if I live to see the day I return to North Carolina, I will suck the hearts blood of the perpetrator. That man and myself cannot stay on the same earth together.

Was she seduced, raped, robbed, impregnated, or something else? We will probably never know.

Other letters are simply humorous, made so by both content and writing style, as was the letter of Confederate soldier Daniel Smith to his brother,

Thomas. Following a variation on the common opening of "I have taken pen in hand to write a few lines," and with one illegible passage of a few words thereafter, he said:

> You know how everything is about a camp and it isn't worth while for me to write about that. ——our old General dose it well tell you how he dose it gard mount. He has all the musitionsers there with the last old drum and old horn they is in the Brigade and he him self come out ever morning and walks along the line just a snorting and a puffing and if a man turns his head the least bit he is right at them and will take holt of there head and straten it and if there feat is not placed just right he will paw their feat with his like a mad bull and you just ought to hear him cuss them sergeants and corporals so I won't say anything. . . .

The first three historic letters I acquired, in 1977, seemed collectible due to their covers, or envelopes, but it was their content that set me, thereafter, on the path of collecting more, searching in each for some bit of charm, some snapshot of another era that would make it a prize.

Those three were written in May and June of 1864 by a young lady named Ellen to her "darling Charlie." She was living near Gainesville, Alabama, with friends named Robinson. Her father was "stationed" in Selma, Alabama, and she mentioned traveling to Macon, Mississippi. Gainesville and Macon are both near the Alabama-Mississippi border, and both are located on the Noxubee River. Selma was the site of the construction and launching of the Confederate naval ram *Tennessee*, which occurred on May 20, 1864. The city was also heavily entrenched and was the site of a cavalry battle on April 2, 1865.

The man to whom Ellen wrote the letters was a Confederate soldier named Charles B. Hamilton, and she addressed them to him "c/o Major E. H. Janney, Gen. R. E. Lee's Hd. Qtrs., Army of Northern Virginia." Based on the content of the letters and her style of writing, it is safe to assume that Ellen was in the age range of sixteen to eighteen, whereas Charlie turned out to be twenty-eight years old.

The letters are noteworthy for two reasons. The first is that they were addressed to General Lee's headquarters. At the time I purchased them I

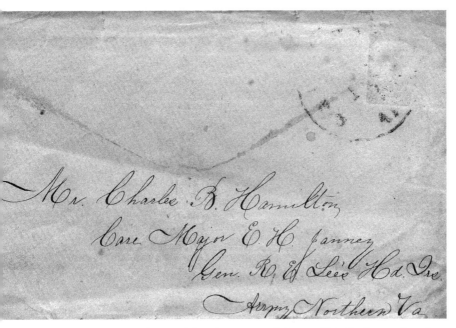

Envelope, or "cover," for one of three letters to Confederate soldier Charles Hamilton, from Ellen, addressed to him at "Gen. R. E. Lee's Hd. Qrs." c. 1864. Image owned by author.

suspected that young Ellen was so optimistically naïve that she believed she could simply address the letters to General Lee's headquarters and that they would somehow filter their way down the ranks to Charlie. Later I discovered that the address was correct, because Charlie was working there, serving under his brother-in-law, Major Eli Janney, who was an assistant quartermaster on General Lee's staff.

The second and more captivating aspect of the letters is a slip of Ellen's pen in one of them, and the consequences that her brief instant of poor penmanship may have caused. It was this minor error that caused me to hire a professional genealogist to try to learn more about the two correspondents and to publish a magazine article about what she found.

Hamilton originally enlisted in the 17th Virginia Infantry on July 19, 1861. His brother, Eli Hamilton, was a captain in the 39th Virginia Cavalry. The same month that Charlie enlisted, the warring armies occupied the Hamilton family's land near Fairfax, Virginia, destroying all of their farm buildings and fences and forcing them to move, under the care of another brother, Enos, to Fauquier County, Virginia. It isn't absolutely clear when Charlie joined his brother-in-law at Lee's headquarters, but the Hamilton and Janney families were very close, having intermarried on more than one occasion, and Janney was appointed to the staff position under Lee in February 1864. It is logical to assume that Charlie joined him shortly thereafter, but service records suggest it may have been as much as a year before, while Janney was serving elsewhere.

The content of the letters makes it clear that Ellen wrote other messages to Charlie in addition to the three I acquired, and that Charlie wrote letters to her, although not as often as she preferred, none of which are known to have survived. Examples of Ellen's attitude and prattle include the following excerpts:

> May 23, 1864: My Darling Charlie: You must dear Charlie excuse all mistakes that occur in this letter for Emma and Miss Robinson are making such a fuss I can hardly hear myself talk. They have told me about one hundred messages to tell you but they are only jealous because they have not such a nice sweet-heart as my dear Charlie and both are quarreling who shall be your second wife.

*   *   *

> Have you sent your Photograph yet? How I long to get it every day. I think I will get a letter but I have been dissatisfied. I know you have written and I hope I will get it soon.
>
> Please dear Charlie keep out of danger for the only thing I have to look forward to is to think you are spared. I do not care to live when God has taken you. Life would have no charm for me and all would be a blank.
>
> I have been dying dear Charlie to have my Photograph taken but Gainseville [sic] can not afford an artist but I expect I will have to go to Macon, Miss. soon and I will have it taken then. You have not told me what kind of dress you like. Let me know and I will go by your orders.
>
> Father asked me not long ago, who I was engaged to. I of course would not tell him. He told me he wanted me to be the old maid of the family but I could not agree to that. What do you say? He is stationed in Selma now and I am out in these old woods ten miles from

any town but I am boarding with a very pleasant family. Mr. Robinson seems more like a father then a stranger. Emma says what has become of her sweet-heart you gave her as she is very anxious to know all about him.

I went to a Pic Nic yesterday, danced all the time and on —— brand ——. Did you ever hear of such a thing but I had a pleasant time. Every one out here is so dull and tame. I don't like them. The young men imagine every young lady he sees looking at him she is dead in love. They don't like me much, say I am too candid for them.

Well dear Charlie I must say good night for my candle is most out. Good bye dear one and write often to one that loves you dearly.—Ellen

May 25, 1864: It seems almost impossible for me to wait until winter before I see you can't you come before that—since it seems years since I last saw you and it has only been five months.

* * *

I have just received your letter dated April 20th. I cannot imagine what made it so long coming, about a month. Last night I wrote you but I could not resist the temptation to write again. I was surprised to hear your brother knew any thing about me. I thought only ladies told their secrets. I am glad your sex have the same failings.

Why Charlie you are not jealous. You must leave all bad habits for me. I have been dying to beg Mother to let me come to Charlotte and I think she has about consented. If she will let me go will you come on to see me? You could run off. Yes, I know you will come.

June 20, 1864: This is the third letter I have written and as yet I have not received a line from you. What can be the matter. Are you sick or what is this reason?

I have been sick from frolicking on Saturday. I rode forty five miles horse back. I went to Macon Mississippi did not return home until ten o'clock at night. We had eight in the party. I tried to have my Photograph taken but could not.

* * *

You can not imagine what a comfort your Photograph is to me in my lonely hours. I imagine it is my own dear Charlie talking to me. I keep it in my Bible so I can kiss it every night and morning. I won't tell you how many times during the day for it would make you vain.

*   *   *

I expect to attend a wedding soon. The groom is about eighty years old and the bride only eighteen but the old man is very rich which of course hides a multitude of faults—and thinks she will be an old man's darling but I prefer to be a young man's slave as the old saying is.

The slip of Ellen's pen occurred in the last of the three letters, in a paragraph that followed her report that she had not been able to have her photograph taken. It was written about the time Lee's army was limping into the lines protecting Petersburg from the advancing Army of the Potomac under General Grant. The Army of Northern Virginia had just survived six weeks of the hardest fighting of the war, with the battles of the Wilderness, Spotsylvania, and Cold Harbor coming one after the other, interspersed with hard marching and a great deal of suffering. Even in his position of relative protection at Lee's headquarters, it is reasonable to imagine that Charlie endured great privation and may have been hanging onto life by his fingernails. Thus one can speculate about what entered his mind when he read the beginning of that short paragraph:

> What do you do with your self these long summer days? I don't do any thing but eat and sleep. I am getting so fat you will not know me and so ugly I am ashamed to look at myself for I am sure I would brake the glass. How much do you think I weigh?

She then answered her own question, and that is where the slip of the pen occurred. I have shown the letter and pointed out the words to hundreds of people over the thirty-plus years I've owned the letters, and with rare exception, each person reads her words exactly as I initially read them and how Charlie must surely have understood them when he read the letter in 1864.

Ellen meant to answer herself by saying "one hundred and twenty pounds what a large lady." Instead, the lower case "t" at the beginning of

Page from letter from Ellen dated June 20, 1864, in which the young lady intended to tell her "Darling Charlie" that she had filled out to 120 pounds, but by which she almost certainly communicated 170 pounds. Image owned by author.

"twenty" is wider than normal and the first half of the next letter, "w" joins the "t" at its base so that the letter looks like an upper case "S." The cross to the "t" does not intersect that letter as it should, but is inserted as a dash a quarter of an inch further to the right, so that the word "twenty" looks exactly like the word "Seventy."

Charlie had not seen Ellen for five months. He was about ten years older and certainly more experienced in the ways of the world and of war than she. He probably wasn't in a great frame of mind just then, and he may have been growing weary of her girlish prattle about picnics and dances, her nagging that he write more and send a photo, her accusations that he was jealous, her suggestion that he should desert the army to come see her, and the not-so-subtle hints that he should propose marriage. To learn that the wench had also gained about fifty-five pounds in less than six months just may have been the last straw.

The genealogist I hired, Marie Melchiori, was quite successful tracking down Charlie. However, having no last name to go on, she struck out with Ellen. She was able to confirm, however, that Charlie and Ellen did not marry. In fact, when Charlie died in 1881, at the age of forty-four, he died a bachelor.[6]

Perhaps Charlie read "one hundred and seventy" in the words intended as "one hundred and twenty" or perhaps not. Perhaps he never wrote Ellen again as a result but perhaps not. We'll never know, and it is a bit shallow-minded to so speculate, but it is compelling, even fun.

It is legal to claim ownership of the foregoing letters and other historic artifacts but only in a trustee status. They are to be admired, preserved, and passed along to the next generation of collectors, to show to friends and other collectors, perhaps increasingly as an example of the quaint manner in which people once communicated. Once, long before technology and electronics made communication instant and of small significance, they were longed for and cherished. Now, even though long ago forgotten by their own writers, many represent those writers' most lasting fame.

5

The Rebel Yell

Even when I am gone, I shall remain in people's minds the star of their rights,
my name will be the war cry of their efforts, the motto of their hopes.
NAPOLEON BONAPARTE

NEAR THE END OF THE 1956 MOVIE *FRIENDLY PERSUASION*, STARRING
Gary Cooper, Dorothy McGuire, and Anthony Perkins, as the home guard
militia lies waiting in ambush for the invading rebels, one of the home
guardsmen lets out a sort of scream, or screech, to which the Yankee officer
commanding shouts angrily "Who gave that Rebel Yell?"

My family went to that movie not long after it was released, although it
may have been 1957 by the time it made it to Shattuck, Oklahoma, Higgins,
Texas, or another theater near home, and I couldn't have been more than
six years old when we saw it. Still, it was and is such a fine, fine movie that
I remember seeing it the first time, and my wife and I now own a copy of
the DVD. It is almost certain that that movie was also the first time I learned
there was such a thing as the Rebel Yell.

The Yell is one of the enduring legends of the War Between the States.
Various primary and secondary sources declare that the sound made by

victorious Confederate soldiers was so singularly unique, so unforgettable, so commanding, that some federal units became demoralized and fled when they first heard it. Other, equally romantic accounts speak of southern units competing to be the "best yelling regiment" in their brigade or to become known as a "good yelling unit." Douglass Southall Freeman, biographer of Lee and author of *Lee's Lieutenants,* once described it as "the pibroch of Southern fealty." A "pibroch" is a musical piece, usually for the bagpipe, usually martial. "Fealty" refers to absolute loyalty, as that of a vassal to a feudal lord.

The Yell was best known as being shouted by Confederates when they charged or were winning a fight, but it had other uses. It is said that units would often take it up while they were on the march, passing it from unit to unit down the road. When anyone in the pre-Chancellorsville Second Corps heard it from afar, soldiers would supposedly declare "It's Jackson, or a rabbit," because the sight of either one would cause the men to start hollering. On one occasion during the Valley Campaign, while the Stonewall Brigade was in camp, one of its five regiments began yelling. Soon another regiment took it up, and then another, and another, until each member of the entire brigade was delivering the Yell at the top of his lungs. General Jackson came out of his tent, leaned on a fence, and listened. The cacophony continued for several moments and then began dying away. When the last echo had rebounded from the Blue Ridge, old Blue Light, universally known to be totally tone deaf, turned toward his tent and said, "That was the sweetest music I ever heard."

Some attempts to describe, and there were a lot, provide colorful description but leave the reader only slightly educated about the actual sound. Following are some of the better first-person accounts:

> Then arose that do-or-die expression, that maniacal maelstrom of
> sound; that penetrating, rasping, shrieking, blood-curdling noise that
> could be heard for miles and whose volume reached the heavens—
> such an expression as never yet came from the throats of sane men,
> but from men whom the seething blast of an imaginary hell would not
> check while the sound lasted.
>
> Confederate Colonel Keller Anderson of Kentucky's Orphan Brigade

At first [the Rebel Yell sounded] like the rumbling of a distant train, it came rushing down the lines like the surging waves upon the ocean, increasing in loudness and grandeur, and passing, it could be heard dying on the left in the distance. Again it was heard coming from the right to die away again on the distant left. It was renewed three times, each with renewed vigor. It was a yell like the defiant tones of a thunderstorm.

   Unknown Confederate soldier after the Battle of the Wilderness

The peculiarity of the Rebel Yell is worthy of mention, but none of the old soldiers who once heard it will ever forget it. Instead of the deep-seated manly cheer of the Union men, the rebel yell was a falsetto yelp which, when heard at a distance, reminded one of a lot of school boys at play. It was a peculiar affair for a battle yell, but though we made fun of it at first, we grew to respect it before the war is over. The yell might sound effeminate, but those who uttered it were not effeminate by any means. When the Union men charged, it was heads erect, shoulders squared and thrown back, and with a firm stride, but when the Johnnies charged, it was with a jog trot in a half bent position, and though they might be met with heavy and blighting volleys, they came on with the pertinacity of bulldogs, filling up gaps and trotting on with their never-ceasing "ki-yi" until we found them face to face.

   Gilbert Adams Hays, Federal soldier

It was the ugliest sound any mortal ever heard.

   Ambrose Bierce, Federal soldier/author/journalist

The Southern troops, when charging, or to express their delight, always yell in a manner peculiar to themselves. The Yankee cheer is much more like ours; but the Confederate officers declare that the Rebel yell has a particular merit, and always produces a salutary and useful effect upon their adversaries. A Corps is sometimes spoken of as a "good yelling regiment."

   Arthur Freemantle, an English officer, accompanying
   Lee's army in the Gettysburg Campaign

And the Rebs a yelling as they came up on the charge with that peculiar yell they have. It sounds like a lot of school boys just let loose.

Samuel Bradbury, Federal engineer

The vigorous manly cheers of the Northern soldiers, so different from the shrill yell of the Rebels.

George T. Stevens, Federal soldier

The shrill yells of the Rebels, mingled with the hoarser cheers of our own men.

Newton Kirk, Federal soldier

Suddenly out of the dusk in front, and to the rear of us, burst the Ki-yi Ki-yi close to us and with it the Rebels were seen.

a doctor of the 4th New York regiment

A single long cry as from the leader of a pack of hounds . . . a dry harsh quality that conveys an uncompromising hostility . . . a howl, a hoarse battle-cry, a cheer, and a congratulation, all in one.

Sidney Lanier, Confederate soldier/poet

It paragons description, that yell! How it starts deep and ends high, how it rises into three increasing crescendos and breaks with a command of battle.

New Orleans Times Picayune reporter

When they got close enough they screamed that woman-like scream and with fixed bayonet on they came.

a Pennsylvanian infantryman

They charged with the invariable yei, yei, yei of the Rebel [Yell].

a Federal newspaperman at the Battle of Hatcher's Run

Yet another person who heard it said it was "a kind of scream . . . like a terrible bull, with a kind of neigh mixed along with it, and it was nearly as loud as a steam whistle." James Ervin Spivey, a soldier in the 26th Georgia, became famous in both the Army of Northern Virginia and the Army of the Potomac for his version of the Yell and was called "Georgia Bull" by his comrades and "Gordon's Bull" by the Federals.

So just what did that sweetest music/ugliest sound any mortal ever heard actually sound like? What was the exact pronunciation, accenting, spelling, and grammar of the Rebel Yell? Was it the "yee-haw" produced in various Civil War movies? Was it the Ki-yi-yi sound described more than once, or was it something else, something more? Was it a specific, definable, unique cry, or was it something more generic, magnified in effect and reputation by thousands of voices, the sweetness of victory, the embroidery of memory, and the veil of years?

Specificity came from an unexpected source. In the mid-fifties, a humorist named H. Allen Smith went on a sort of literary hunt across the South, collecting different versions of the Yell from people—none veterans of the war—who were arguably in a position to know what it sounded like. His book, *The Rebel Yell*, was published by Doubleday in 1955 and was intended as whimsical satire. It contains many limping anecdotes and cornball witticisms; their ability to invoke mirth did not survive the decade of the 1950s. However, tucked among the cuteness are no less than nine candidates for the Yell's exact pronunciation.

The first—"Eee-Yow!"—came from a 1952 *Time* magazine article. The next—"Keeook"—was provided by a northern scoutmaster whose only credentials were that his Panther patrol used the same cry on Boy Scout outings. Historian James Street authoritatively offered "Rrrrrr-yahhhhhhhhh-yip-yip-yip-yip-yip" as the true Yell, although he was also heard to emit it as "Yeeeeeeeeeeeow!" during a post-party argument with a Chapel Hill shoe merchant over its correct sound. The merchant claimed the true sound was "Whooooooooooooooo-wow!" In Charleston, a lawyer considered an expert on the Yell offered "Yuhhhhh-wooooooooo-eeeeeee-UH!" Douglass Southall Freeman, who should have known if anyone did, delivered it as "Yeeeeeeeeee-ahhhhhhhhhhhh!" When Smith published a newspaper article on the subject, he was challenged by the *Twin City Sentinel*, which claimed "Eeeeeeee-YUH-haaeeeeooooooooo." Finally, composer Richard Bales offered "Ooooooo-eeeeeeee!"

Mercifully, someone with better credentials and experience also offered an exact spelling and pronunciation of the Yell. Colonel Harvey Dew of the 9th Virginia Cavalry, who surely heard the sound repeatedly in his war days under J.E.B. Stuart, carefully recorded it's intonation as it was given by his regiment during a charge at the Battle of Brandy Station. Writing in an April 1892 article in *Century Illustrated* magazine, he said:

> In an instant every voice with one accord vigorously shouted the "Rebel yell," which was so often heard on the field of battle. "Woh-who-ey! who-ey! who-ey! Woh-who-ey! who-ey!" etc. [The best illustration of this "true yell" which can be given the reader is by spelling it as above, with directions to sound the first syllable "woh" short and low and the second "who" with a very high and prolonged note deflecting upon the third syllable "ey."]

For those of you who want to try the Dew version of the Yell at home, note that "deflect" means "to bend or turn to one side, to swerve."

Modern versions or guesstimates of the Yell have been recorded many times. One not deserving of notice was done during the Civil War Centennial for an album of southern music titled *The Confederacy.* The composer was Richard Bales, one of H. Allen Smith's demonstrators, and his "Oooo-eeeey" is contained at the end of the last track of the album as background for the concluding strains of "Dixie." It can best be described as somebody's impression of a windy night. A better version was inserted into another set of Centennial Civil War LPs (labeled as standing for "Living Presence") recordings titled *The Civil War: Its Music and Sounds* by Frederick Fennel. The two-record set contains bugle calls, martial music, and drum and fife tunes on three of its four sides, and the "sounds of conflict" on the other, which consists of a narrated account of the war from Fort Sumter to Gettysburg, complete with recordings of period weapons and cannons being fired on actual battlefields. At the climax of Pickett's Charge, as the Confederates break through the Union lines, a scattering of high-pitched yells and cries captures a noise many folks might have made, heard, or identified as the Rebel Yell.

There are, however, a handful of recordings with better credentials, having been made of actual Confederate veterans providing their rendition of the famous battle cry. One came from the seventy-fifth anniversary of the Battle of Gettysburg. During a newsreel filming of the obligatory handshake across the wall by veterans of both sides, six or eight Confederates took up the Yell. It was sort of a high-pitched "Wa-woo-woohoo, wa-woo woohoo" delivered by gentlemen in their nineties.[7] It sounds similar to the Yell described by Harvey Dew, though understandably lacking the hostility, defiance, and blood-curdling quality described by wartime witnesses.

One might forego further speculation about the sound of the Yell at this point and be content that the question is resolved, both audibly and graphically. However, the other recordings, once they finally became available, have rendered further speculation inevitable.

The *Confederate Veteran* magazine reported on more than one occasion that a recording of the Yell was planned or had been made. The best candidate was made at a convention of the United Daughters of the Confederacy, probably in Florida in or about 1898. However, if made and if preserved, the location of that particular version is unknown.

The recording that attracted my attention, sometime in the early 1980s, was not the next one in chronological order but was probably one that generated the most publicity. William Randolph Hearst's motion picture company, Cosmopolitan Pictures, decided to make a Civil War movie called *Operator 13*, just as the seventy-fifth anniversary of the war was approaching in 1934. It was to star Gary Cooper and Marion Davies and was to include a genuine Rebel Yell, as rendered by a genuine Rebel.

A veteran named Sampson S. Simmons, late of Company E, 8th Virginia Calvary, who was an active member of the United Confederate Veterans, agreed to provide the authentic Yell and did so. I read about this in a magazine article somewhere, and when I later saw the old motion picture was going to be shown on television, I watched and recorded it, curious to hear what Simmons produced. I was disappointed. There was no Rebel Yell in the movie.

The article about the making of the movie reported that Simmons's recording was presented to and preserved by the United Daughters of the Confederacy, so I decided to contact the UDC headquarters in Richmond, Virginia, and find out if it was possible to obtain a copy. In a series of phone calls and a letter, I was able to ascertain that the recording did exist, but I was never connected with nor did I receive a call or letter back from anyone with the UDC who had authority to either allow or deny permission for me to hear or copy it.

I then learned from an article in the *Confederate Veteran* that the UDC had voted at another convention in Florida in 1931 "to have the Rebel Yell preserved for posterity by means of a Victrola record." The Yell was then given by a small group of veterans and probably recorded at a subsequent UDC convention in New Orleans in 1932. It appeared that the UDC might be the owner of at least two recordings of the real Yell.

In 1998, a fellow Yell enthusiast and I connected on the Internet, and we decided to make a two-pronged assault on the UDC headquarters in Richmond. The result was the same. The ladies acknowledged their possession of a recording but indicated that they had no equipment to play it, either saying or suggesting that it was preserved on a wax cylinder. When we offered to secure the necessary equipment in return for a chance to hear the recording, communication from the UDC ceased. They did not seem anxious to share what they "preserved for posterity" with those of us who make up that posterity.

However, shortly after the beginning of the twenty-first century, another recording of a Confederate veteran giving the Yell was posted on the Internet at the website of the 26th North Carolina, a re-enactor unit, for all the world to hear. It was made in 1935 when Thomas Alexander, formerly of the 37th North Carolina Infantry and then ninety years old, allowed a radio station—WBT of Charlotte, North Carolina—to record his rendition. That version sounds no more like Harvey Dew's version than California resembles Connecticut. It is more of a loud, high bark. It was then re-recorded in multiple duplicates by History Publishing of New York to produce an imitation of what a Confederate company might have sounded like while attacking.[8]

In the meantime, I served as a Confederate staff officer in the 125th anniversary re-enactment of the Battle of Chickamauga and took advantage of the opportunity to distribute copies of the Harvey Dew article to the members of the brigade commanded by re-enactor Charles Clark. After some discussion and coaching at dress parade, the brigade then attempted the Yell in battle. It sounded pretty good, and a few seconds of the brigade's impression were captured on the Classic Images video of the re-enactment.

Much of the foregoing was contained in an article I wrote for the newsletter of Company D of the 27th Virginia, another re-enactment unit, that was posted on the Internet and repeated on yet another website. That article

"That's the Rebel Yell," a Confederate veteran tells the camera man in 1938, after he and his companions gave a geriatric version of the battle cry, caught in a video of Union and Confederate veterans meeting at the wall which Pickett charged on July 3, 1863, at the seventy-fifth anniversary of the Battle of Gettysburg. Courtesy of William B. Styple, *Echoes of the Blue & Gray*, Volume II, Kearny, NJ: Bell Grove Publishing Co. 1990.

came to the attention of National Public Radio in mid-2007, when someone there decided to do a short article about the Yell for the June 2, 2007, episode of *Weekend America*. A reporter, Amy Scott, called me on the phone, explained what she was doing, and asked if I would agree to be interviewed about the Yell. I eagerly, and foolishly, jumped at the chance.

I should have known better, but I didn't. I thought they were doing a serious piece and had singled me out as a talking head on the esoteric topic. I expected to dazzle them with my expertise. My dazzle turned out to include a generous amount of fizzle.

The interview, which was recorded for future editing, went fine, but at the end, inevitably, Ms. Scott asked me to attempt my version of the Yell for the radio audience. I had been afraid this would happen, not only because it was obvious it would and that I would sound like an idiot but because, at age fifty-six, my vocal chords and lungs could not possibly do the Yell justice. Nevertheless, I blared out a sort of Harvey Dew/Georgia Bull rendition that, in retrospect, sounds a lot like a very upset or possibly oversexed burro.

I expected and hoped that the kind Ms. Scott would not be tempted to use this freely given piece of blackmail material to my disadvantage. Au contraire. The radio program led with it in a manner that seemed to illustrate what wackos who think this silly sort of thing is important will come up with if left unattended. Major ouch.

In 2008, I received an e-mail from a man named Terryl W. Elliott, who told me he was in the process of writing a book about the Yell. He had seen my article on the Internet and had tracked me down, partly to get permission to quote portions of it and partly to compare notes. We talked. He revealed that he had attempted to locate the war record of Harvey Dew, the veteran who described the Yell in print in 1892, and had discovered that his name was apparently Harvey Drew, instead of Dew.

I gave him the permission he sought. Later he called to tell me that the Museum of the Confederacy in Richmond had recently released a recording of the Yell, available on CD for sale online. The MOC obviously held more sway with the UDC than I had, and the long-anticipated recording made for the movie *Operator 13* had been released, played, and re-recorded for the entire world to hear. I immediately ordered the CD, titled *The Rebel Yell Lives.*

The CD begins with a playing of the Richard Bales version of *Dixie,* continues with an imitation of the Yell, provides a short narrated history of it, and then plays the Thomas Alexander version, recorded in 1935. After a pause, the question is asked whether listeners can rely on that version, which is nothing like the Dew/Drew or Gettysburg seventy-fifth anniversary renderings, as being authentic. The CD answers its own question by proudly presenting its flagship Yell, recorded by S. S. Simmons for the movie *Operator 13* on April 10, 1934, and later given for safekeeping to the United Daughters of the Confederacy.

The Simmons recording does not sound a little like the Alexander version; it sounds *exactly* like the Alexander version. Instead of a yip yip yip or a who-whooey, it is the same high, rough, ugly, staccato bark that Alexander provided, as it turns out, a year later than Simmons. It was something that can understandably be characterized as the "ugliest sound any mortal ever heard," particularly if the person doing the characterizing despised those who were uttering it, as did Ambrose Bierce.

This means, of course, that the Alexander/Simmons versions, which are actual recordings of actual Confederate veterans, are the nearest sounds available today to the "true" Rebel Yell, even though the sound is very little like the Dew/Drew/Gettysburg seventy-fifth/Monte Akers imagined versions. That doesn't explain how two men in the same cavalry corps of the same Army of Northern Virginia—Harvey Drew and S. S. Simmons— heard and yelled such remarkably different battle cries and called them by the same name, but when the Museum of the Confederacy and the United Daughters of the Confederacy are in agreement on a subject, an amateur historian should not voice a dissenting opinion too loudly if he wishes to have credibility.

Then in January 2010, I received from its author a copy of the newly published *"Dammit, Holler' 'em Across:" The History of the Rebel Yell*, by the aforesaid Terry Elliott. The title of the book was selected from a statement made by the irascible Confederate Lt. General Jubal Anderson Early in May 1864 when he directed soldiers that were nearly out of ammunition to substitute the Yell for bullets, which they supposedly did with success.

The book is extremely well-written and thorough, tracing potential roots of the Yell back to Scots-Irish roots in the seventeenth century, including most of the information provided in this chapter, plenty more, numerous quotations from across the decades since the Civil War about the sound or purpose of the Yell, illustrations that include a photo of Thomas Alexander, and no less than seven poems about it, including my own. Anyone desiring more information on this esoteric subject will not find a more authoritative analysis.

Terry Elliott's book arrived just as *The Accidental Historian* was about to go to copyediting, and this chapter was revised to include the foregoing discussion of *Holler' 'em Across*. No sooner had that been accomplished, however, then Terry e-mailed to let me know that another recording of the Yell had surfaced, after which he sent a copy of it.

It was neither the Rosetta Stone nor the Holy Grail of Rebel Yell recordings. In fact, it shed more dark than light on its exact sound but may explain why the Simmons and Alexander versions of the Yell sound so similar—because they may be the same yell produced by the same (old) yeller.

Rather than trying to piece the story together thirdhand, I asked Terry Elliott if he would be willing to supply the information he possessed for inclusion in this chapter. He agreed and provided the following:

> One thing about the Rebel Yell—not unlike the rest of history—is that just about the time you think you're getting a handle on it along comes some new discovery or information of some sort, which then has to be taken into consideration and accounted for. And, generally speaking, this new knowledge seems to raise more questions than it answers.
>
> This is the case with the recorded versions of the Rebel Yell. We have the excellent CD released by the Museum of the Confederacy,

The Rebel Yell Lives!, which incorporates the Alexander/WBT recording and the Simmons/UDC recording along with several enhanced
versions to simulate increasingly larger units. All of this appeared to be
on solid footing, and indeed might have been the final word. After all,
the two were so similar to one another that they each appeared to corroborate the sound and authenticity of the other. Plus, the provenance
for each recording was apparently spotless. But now some new, or at
least previously uncirculated, information has surfaced that is causing
some concern and questions.

In communications recently with Waite Rawls and John Coski at
the Museum of the Confederacy (they are the president and historian
respectively and the folks responsible for the Rebel Yell CD) and also
with Clint Johnson, a Civil War author, historian and re-enactor with
the 26th North Carolina (he was one of the people initially involved
in bringing the Alexander recording to light and putting it on the 26th
N.C. site), and based on these contacts, this is how I piece the story and
situation together:

Clint Johnson and Ken Curtis (a fellow re-enactor) became aware
of the recording of Alexander from his grandson, J.B. Joye, about ten
years ago.—The family story was that at some point after the recording was made in 1935 a request was made to WBT for a copy which
was furnished to them on some medium (possibly a record or some
type of reel-to-reel recording.) This was eventually transferred to a
cassette tape, which is what J.B. Joye possessed.—Johnson and Curtis received Joye's permission to copy it and post it on their website.
There were three parts to the recording: An interview with Alexander,
a Rebel Yell by a group of old veterans, and Alexander's solo Yell. According to Clint, at that time there was no MP3, and digital recording
was difficult to do and post, so the decision was made to post only the
solo Yell. At that point there was some rumored knowledge of the
other two parts, but most people (myself included) hadn't ever heard
them and didn't know if they actually existed.

As time went by, the solo version of the Yell spread to various locations on the web and finally the folks at the MOC got it and started a
proactive approach to enhance and disseminate it, eventually resulting
in their CD. Of course, as previously stated, the CD also included the
Simmons/UDC solo recording of the Yell. There's no need to go into

the whole story again here, but suffice it to say that Waite Rawls had all he could handle prying the recording from the well-meaning grasp of the ladies at the UDC.

Rawls and Coski were elated to have the "confirming" Simmons recording and, as indicated, proceeded with the production of the CD. In the year or so since its release their initial elation has been tempered by a gnawing concern: The two versions of the Yell were almost *too* similar! Some fairly elementary audio testing was conducted and it was discovered that each recording was exactly twenty seconds in length. In addition, both are comprised of a repeating pattern of the "yelp" which makes up the total Yell. Each pattern has two short yelps followed by a longer yelp, which has three secondary parts to it. This pattern is repeated six times in each recording. Furthermore, there are slight variations during the repeated patterns. Between patterns two and three and patterns four and five there is a slightly longer pause than between the other patterns. Also, four of the short yelps have a lower and slightly gruffer quality to them. The point of interest here is that each of these variations occurs identically in both recordings. The implication here is fairly obvious: the two recordings may be one in the same!

When the recordings of the Alexander interview and the veteran's group Yell became more widely known and readily available because of digital technology, some new concerns were added to the mix. The Alexander interview reveals a fairly spry and somewhat feisty old gentleman, particularly for someone in his nineties, but without a very strong voice. The group Yell is somewhat reminiscent of the Rebel Yell on the newsreel film of the veterans at the Gettysburg reunion; it sounds a little weak and feeble. This, in turn, has led to a new suspicion about the Alexander recording. If his voice, which is so strong on the solo recording, is among those on the group recording, why isn't it more apparent? When this is coupled with the great similarity between the two recordings, the possibility is furthered that they might, in fact, be the same recording.

The Simmons-UDC recording was made in 1934 and the Alexander-WBT recording was made in 1935. The interview and group Yell recording had the Alexander solo Yell spliced onto the end of it. This could be explained in either of two ways: The solo recording was made at a different time and place and thus had to be spliced on later, or possibly the Simmons recording, for some unknown reason, at some unknown point in time, was spliced onto the end and through the years this fact was lost.

There are dozens of potential scenarios that could be proposed to clarify and/or explain these problems, some more dubious and some more likely than others. Some might even raise new questions. Consider the following: What if Alexander didn't join in with his fellow veterans during the group Yell recording? (Maybe he said something like, "That wasn't very good. Take me and your machine to another room and I'll show you how the Rebel Yell really sounded.") What if the Alexander recording was made earlier, in 1929 or 1932, as some sources suggest? Furthermore, what if Simmons, as head of the California Division of the United Confederate Veterans, was aware of the Alexander recording and rather than making a new recording in 1935 he merely acquired a copy of the earlier recording and furnished it to the movie studio? What if there is the possibility that the "Hollywood-made" Simmons recording could have been enhanced by the studio at time it was made? Certainly this case could have many more "what-ifs."

Another interesting point concerning the authenticity of this version of the Rebel Yell, wherever and from whomever it may have originated, is testimony from many re-enactors who have switched to this form of the Yell. Waite Rawls, John Coski, and Clint Johnson all assure me that the "modern Confederates" all report that they found it easier to do on the double-quick run than what they had been doing previously.

The best we can do at this point is to appreciate, even treasure, what recorded history of the Rebel Yell we now have available and let any future "audio forensic analysis" sort out the details. After all, half of the joy of history is speculating about the unknown aspects of it![9]

About the Yell, I suspect that beyond the fact that it was high-pitched, or falsetto, that its spelling and phonetics were probably less important for producing the "true" sound than was the amount of adrenaline that supported its emission. Different units and armies and even different individuals apparently gave different versions of the Yell. Its origin has been attributed to Texans imitating an Indian war cry, to Virginians giving the fox-hunt cry, and to backwoods coon hunters repeating their cry to the hounds. All of those attributions are probably correct. At the time the Yell became famous, its sponsors were simply yelling in an excited manner, the way all soldiers have yelled from time immemorial, and the yell they selected was surely the same one they used back home when they were excited.

Why should they have all given the exact same sound? J.E.B. Stuart's cavalry almost certainly sounded like Harvey Dew describes and perhaps a lot of Lee's entire army did also but apparently not all of it, considering that both Thomas Alexander and Sampson Simmons were part of that army. What of the Army of Tennessee and those in the Trans-Mississippi? They were yelling long before anyone from Virginia came out west to teach them how to do it the way they did it back east. As the war progressed and the Yell became more famous, its sound probably became more standardized, but a final contender for the most genuine was never selected.

As Douglass Southall Freeman told H. Allen Smith, "The rebel yell is pure legend. In Richmond it goes one way. In Atlanta you'll hear another. In Birmingham still another."

Despite Chickamauga, recordings, the Internet, and NPR, however, I believe that I once came close to hearing the—or a—*real* Rebel Yell. It was at the filming of the movie *Gettysburg* in 1992. Troy Cool, sometime member of the Stonewall Brigade and the Southern Guard, was working full time for Turner films, and one day when the re-enactor extras, including me, were portraying Confederates, someone asked Troy to demonstrate the Yell during a lull in the filming.

After a few seconds of preparation, he did. It was the Harvey Dew version, but he went far beyond Dew's ability to describe or General Clark's Chickamauga brigade's ability to imitate and even way beyond, I believe, the Thomas Alexander–Sampson Simmons embellished and multiplied recording version. He reached down into his gut and screeched it as loudly and with as much desperate, penetrating force as the original Confederates must have produced while coming through a hailstorm of lead and seeing that they were winning another battle. My curiosity was sated.

Predictably, I also wrote a poem about the subject sometime in the mid-1980s. It was posted on the Internet by the Stonewall Brigade and has been picked up and reprinted at a few other websites, causing me to believe it resonated with a few other folks who care about the Yell:

THE REBEL YELL

None of us have ever heard it.
None of us ever will.
There's no one left who can give it.
Tho you may hear its echo still.

You may hear it up near Manassas,
and down around Gaines Mill.
In December it echoes in Fredericksburg,
in May around Chancellorsville

It's the "pibroch of Southern fealty."
It's a Comanche brave's battle cry.
It's an English huntsman's call to the hounds.
It's a pig farmer's call to the sty.

It's a high-pitched trilling falsetto.
It's the yip of a dog in flight.
It's the scream of a wounded panther.
It's the shriek of the wind in the night.

It was yelled when the boys flushed a rabbit.
It was passed man to man in the ranks.
It was cheered when they saw their leaders.
It was screamed when they whipped the Yanks.

But none of us will ever hear it.
Tho some folks mimic it well.
No soul alive can truly describe
the sound of the Rebel Yell.

6

Recuerde el libro del Alamo

*If it was just me, simple old David from Tennessee, I might drop over that wall some
night, take my chances. But that Davy Crockett feller . . .
they're all watchin' him.*

DAVID CROCKETT

as portrayed by Billy Bob Thornton, in *The Alamo* (Disney, 2004)

INEVITABLY, THESE TALES MUST TURN TOWARD SAN ANTONIO DE BEXAR
and the dustup that occurred there toward the end of February and beginning of March 1836.

I possess no letters or artifacts to analyze or share about that place, and
my experiences during the filming of the IMAX movie *Alamo: The Price of
Freedom* are discussed in another chapter. The facts of the few tales of the
Alamo I have to share are ones that anyone could have gathered for themselves with a little time and effort, but as I've already managed to herd them
into a little pen, I'll point them out and tell you their names.

The Alamo intrigued me at an early age. What I did about it, besides
visit the place and serve as an extra in a short movie about it, was make it
the focus of a novel I wrote in the early 1990s, that I hoped to get published

but didn't. Nevertheless it will serve as a backdrop for this chapter because it was the background for that novel that led to most of the Alamo stories this chapter contains.

The gist of the story was that one of the combatants in the Alamo, Henry Warnell, managed to escape the battle, wounded, and took with him the flag that flew over the fort during the thirteen days of the siege, before the Mexican army, under Santa Anna, stormed the fortress early the morning of March 6, 1836, killed most of the people inside, and turned the place into an icon of epic proportions. The story then focused on the search for the flag, in modern times, which was simultaneously the object of a quest by an unscrupulous, murderous, artifact collector and a heroic young protagonist and his likeable sidekick who were unwittingly drawn into the quest by clues to its location that fell into the protagonist's hands and that he managed to decipher. There was also a crusty old college professor, who had suspected the existence of the flag ever since being presented with one of the clues decades earlier, and a beautiful, spirited, love-interest woman to help move the plot along, sort of like every history/adventure novel ever written from Indiana Jones to Clive Cussler.

One slightly clever difference that proved not to help get the book published was that it was actually two stories in one. Each chapter had an 1836 portion and a 1996 portion, the earlier one moving backward in time from Warnell's death following the battle, at which time he entrusted the flag to a friend, and the modern one moving forward in time from the initial discovery of the flag's existence toward its recovery, so that both old and new stories ultimately collided, and all the minor and major mysteries are solved and resolved at the end, in a dénouement.

One of the fascinating mysteries of the Alamo, as with the Little Big Horn, is the question of whether any of the men who fought there escaped being killed. Henry Warnell was an actual defender of the mission fort on the San Antonio River, and it is quite conceivable that he did escape—at least one document exists that says he did. He is also one of the few of the rank and file in the little Texian army about whom history has left some blurry snapshot details.

This latter development is so because the Republic of Texas, having no cash or coin to run its infantile government but a ton of wide open spaces, used land to reward its heroes and to attract new settlers. Grants of land

were awarded to the heirs of those who fought at the Alamo and other battles of the Texas Revolution. Such land grants and numerous others from
the Republic of Texas, the Mexican and Spanish governments in earlier days,
and the State of Texas after 1845 were sold, traded, bought, and, shocking
as it may seem, often counterfeited. This latter practice, plus multiple sales
of the same lands, sales by non-owners, intestate deaths, unprobated wills,
simple mistakes, complicated mistakes, and acts of wildly imaginative and
complex fraud, led to a great deal of confusion and competing claims for
the same territory.

To add to the confusion, officials of the Mexican state of Tamaulipas,
which included much of what is now South Texas, had sought to encourage
colonization of its vacant lands through Mexican colonization laws of 1824
and 1825 by issuing numerous land grants, many to local Mexican ranch-
ers. They continued to do so, in the name of the Republic of Mexico, after
1836, when the first Congress of the Republic of Texas declared that the
Texas boundaries extended to the Rio Grande, and they kept at it until 1848,
when the Mexican War ended and the Treaty of Guadalupe Hidalgo officially concluded the boundary dispute with Mexico. The new State of Texas
officially recognized the land grants made under Spanish and Mexican rule
as valid, but that didn't resolve the confusion. So in 1849, Texas Governor
Peter Bell asked the legislature to conduct an investigation of land claims.

In 1850 the legislature instituted a board of commissioners to do so
and appointed William H. Bourland and James B. Miller as its chief commissioners, plus Robert Jones Rivers as the board's attorney. Over the next
two years the commission received testimony, evidence, and affidavits, and
reviewed hundreds of documents in order to decide who did and did not
own a great deal of land in Texas. The commission issued its recommenda-
tions in a document known as the Bourland and Miller Report, now in the
archives of the Texas General Land Office. The report still didn't resolve all
questions, and in February 1860, the legislature turned responsibility for
confirming Spanish and Mexican titles over to the district courts.

Warnell's son, John Warnell, was the recipient of land grants due
to his father's service in the Texas Revolution, and it was one of those
grants that was investigated. Several affidavits concerning Henry were
filed with the commission, including one by Susannah Dickinson, (sometimes spelled Dickerson), who was the widow of Alamo artillery captain

Almeron Dickinson and the mother of Angelina Dickinson, "the Babe of the Alamo."

Henry Warnell was described as twenty-four years old in 1836, small, maybe five-foot-three or -four, and weighing 118 pounds or less. He had blue eyes, red hair, fair skin, freckles, and a knot over one eye. He came to Texas from Arkansas, either Sevier or Crawford County, where his wife, whose name was Lydia Ragsdale, died in childbirth in 1834. After leaving their infant son, John, in the care of a friend, he went to Bastrop and found work with a man named Edward Burleson.

History doesn't record exactly what he did for Burleson, but he was known to have been a "race rider" or jockey, as well as a hunter when he lived in Arkansas. Almost all of the affidavits describe Warnell as being an "incessant" or "extravagant" or "enthusiastic" tobacco-chewer who "sometimes drank whiskey" and who was a "great talker." Such tidbits of information had nothing to do with title to the land, but their inclusion suggests he was colorful and was well-remembered by people who came in contact with him.

Warnell fought in the Alamo as an artilleryman, a gunner, under Captain William R. Carey. Almost half the men in the fort served cannons, and most died beside their guns. Mrs. Dickinson remembered him, mentioned that he was small and light-complexioned, stated she recollected distinctly having seen him in the Alamo about three days prior to its fall, and as none escaped the massacre, she "verily believed he was among the unfortunate number who fell there." What is particularly interesting about her statement is that she also said she recollected hearing Warnell remark how he'd "much rather be out in the open prairie, than to be pent up in that manner."

The heirs of Henry Warnell, represented by Edward Burleson, claimed as much land as the Republic, and later the State of Texas, would award to veterans and heroes of the Revolution. They received not only grants from the Republic but later one from the state in which young John Warnell received two-thirds of a league and a labor of land plus a donation grant of 640 acres based on his father's service at the Alamo.

One or more of the grants awarded prior to 1850 was examined by the Bourland-Miller Commission, and evidence that surfaced as a result suggests that Warnell might have been a genuine survivor of the battle.

On the application of the heirs of Henry Wornell dec'd for bounty & Donation lands.

Personally appeared before me the undersigned authority, Mrs Susannah Hunneck, alias Dickinson, who on oath says; I was in the Alamo prior to, and at its fall, on 6th March 1836, and knew a man there by the name of Henry Wornell; and recollect distinctly having seen him in the Alamo for about three days prior to its fall; and as none escaped the massacre, I verily believe he was among the unfortunate number who fell there, so bravely in the defence of their country. I recollect having heard him remark that he had much rather be out in the open prairie, than to be kept up in that manner. Said Wornell, was a man of rather small stature, light complexion and I think red or sandy hair.

Subscribed by making her mark   Susannah + Hunneck
And sworn to before me, this   her mark
8th March 1860.
                        W. S. Hotchkiss
                        Com. of Claims

Almeron Dickinson

Affidavit dated March 8, 1860, containing the mark of Alamo survivor Susannah Dickinson, then Susannah Hannig (misspelled "Hunneck") in which she testified that she saw Henry Warnell at the Alamo, "and as none escaped the massacre," she believed he fell there. She also recalled hearing him say that "he had much rather be out in the open prairie, than to be pent up in that manner," a remark sometimes attributed to David Crockett. Courtesy of Texas General Land Office.

There's not much to go on, but according to one affidavit in the record, given by a man named Henry Anderson in Belknap, Texas, Warnell was at the "massacre" of the Alamo, was wounded, but escaped to Port Lavaca, where he died in less than three months from the effects of his wounds.

Not a lot is known about Anderson,[10] how he knew Warnell, or whether he was present at his death, nor is there an obvious reason that he had motive to invent such a story, although one can be surmised.

The laws of the Republic of Texas that awarded land for service during the Texas Revolution did not simply declare that every veteran, or the heir of a veteran who was dead, was entitled to a certain number of acres or leagues or labors of land. The laws were worded differently according to the type and length of service rendered, the battle in which the soldier fought, or the campaign in which he participated. With regard to the Alamo, land was awarded to the heirs of the men who died there. If the law was to be applied literally and technically, as is the custom, land was not awarded to someone whose father or husband fought at the Alamo, was mortally wounded, and escaped to die two or three months later. The law required the veteran to die at the Alamo in order for his heir to get land. Dying at Port Lavaca wouldn't count.

So there is a possibility that the Anderson affidavit was a lie, filed on behalf of another claimant. His affidavit does not say that he was under oath or that he had firsthand knowledge about Warnell's death. Instead, it says that he "would respectfully represent" that Warnell was at the Alamo and died at Port Lavaca. However, Anderson signed the affidavit as "Agent for the Heirs," and it is possible that John Warnell sought him out and secured his written statement precisely because Anderson was with Warnell when he died. Henry's heirs were trying to prove that Henry was at the Alamo, and probably no one had thought about how Anderson's affidavit might be applied literally and technically according to the law under which the grant was awarded.

The court ultimately upheld the claim and the validity of the Warnell land grant, but the vote was split, two to one. One of the three judges voted against it and wrote a fourteen-page dissenting opinion containing a litany of legalistic arguments in support of his position. He did not zero in on the Anderson affidavit or say that Warnell did not die in the Alamo on March 6, 1836. Instead, he dissected the different land grant laws and why

To the Hon. Edward Clark,
Commissioner of Claims
Austin, Texas.

The undersigned would respectfully represent, that Henry Warnell, was a soldier under Travis — at the massacre of the Alamo, in the year 1836, in the struggle for Texan Independence; that he was wounded at the said massacre, but made his escape to Port Lavacaa, where he died in less than three months from the effects of said wound. — That he was a single man, and as such entitled to receive a Headright, of one third of a League, a Bounty of 1920 acres, and Donation of 640 acres, Respectfully submitted.

Henry Anderson
Agent for the Heirs.

Sworn to and subscribed before me, In witness whereof I have hereunto subscribed my name and affixed the impress of my official seal, at office in Belknap, this 30th day of July, A.D. 1858.

James H. Swindells.
Notary Public
Young Co. Texas,

Affidavit dated July 30, 1858, of Henry Anderson, "Agent for the Heirs" of Henry Warnell, in which he testified that a wounded Henry Warnell escaped the "massacre of the Alamo" and died at Port Lavaca less than three months after the battle. Courtesy of Texas General Land Office.

each would not apply, based on when Warnell arrived in Texas and whether the ancestor of the claimants "fell with Travis, Fannin, Ward and Johnson," before declaring that "for the foregoing and other reasons which I deem unnecessary to state that the Board created by the Act of 7th February, 1860, has no jurisdiction in the case of the Heirs of Henry Warnell."

No jurisdiction? Other reasons? Was it possible that the judge really wanted John Warnell to keep his land and believed that Henry fought at the Alamo, but he was a stickler who felt compelled to follow the letter of the law and couldn't bear to vote for the validity of the claim if Warnell didn't actually die where the law required him to die?

For this book, I wanted to find support for the idea that Warnell escaped and that the Anderson affidavit was genuine, and I was also intrigued by the concept that the law was applied, or not applied, literally, so that a death during the battle of the Alamo, as opposed by a death caused by the battle, was required in order for an associated land grant to be awarded. It occurred to me that some light might be shed on the matter by looking into the post-battle claims of Brigido Guerrero, to see if any compensation he received for being in the Texas Revolution was based on his service at the Alamo.

The concept that a soldier who fought for Texas independence at the Alamo and survived the battle, other than as a courier who left the fort prior to its fall, has been labeled by one Alamo author as "the Crown Jewel of Texas Legends."[11] Guerrero was apparently just such a survivor, and yet he never received much in the way of crowns or jewels. He is scarcely remembered as having even been there, let alone as a hero.

It should be noted that Brigido Guerrero was not the same man as Jose Maria Guerrero.[12] Both were at the Alamo, and the latter's name is listed as one of those killed on the Alamo monument, or cenotaph, constructed in front of the Alamo in the 1930s, but the inclusion of his name is an error. Jose Maria Guerrero was a member of Juan Seguin's company of Tejano volunteers, but he left the Alamo before the siege began, survived the Revolution, and was awarded a pension for his service during the 1870s.[13]

Brigido Guerrero was a deserter from the Mexican army who, following the defeat of General Cos and seizure of the Alamo in December 1835, threw in with the Texians and fought beside them in the Alamo until March 6, when it became apparent that he was destined to be on the "death" instead of "victory" side of his commanding officer's catch phrase. At that point, he dropped to knees and welcomed the oncoming Mexican *soldados* as liberators, claiming to have been a prisoner of war of the Texians all along. It worked. Not only was Brigido's life spared, but thirty years later he applied for and received a pension from the state of Texas for his service during the Revolution.

However, whether due to his pre- and post-battle association with the enemy or simply because he was not an Anglo, Brigido has been conveniently overlooked by popular history as an Alamo survivor.

As for the point of my inquiry, Guerrero's pension records revealed that, in fact, he did not receive any compensation for being at the Alamo but for other service during the Revolution. That proves nothing, of course, and may even cast doubt on his having been present at the Alamo to be spared by the Mexican soldiers on March 6, 1836, but it was at least consistent with the concept that failing to die at the Alamo was its own reward—it didn't score much in the way of governmental kudos.

Semi-interesting side note: while doing the research for this chapter of the book, both at the Texas General Land Office, where the original affidavits regarding the land grant investigations are located, and at the Texas State Archives, where the Guerrero pension applications are, I had trouble finding information at the latter place and asked one of the archivists a question. When she heard that it involved men who were at the Alamo, she pointed to a man sitting at a table reading some ancient documents and told me, "You ought to ask him. He's writing a book about the men who fought at the Alamo and is one of the leading experts on the subject."

So I ambled over, introduced myself, and struck up a conversation. I'm embarrassed to say now that I can't even recall his name, but I'm sure it is on the spine of a few tomes. He was researching, he told me, the question of exactly how many Texian defenders actually perished in the battle. The commonly accepted number(s), 189, 183, or 181, have a pretty firm basis in things like Travis's letter of February 24, 1836, in which he stated that there were 150 defenders, after which 32 more came in from Gonzales. Messengers came and went. That, plus some post-battle body counting, makes a range of 180 to 190 pretty reliable.

However, at least one Mexican account stated that there were 250 dead defenders. Mexican officials of the day were notoriously careful record-keepers, so this claim was interesting, but scholars generally considered it a miscount attributable to inclusion of some Mexican dead. Some of the latter may have been dressed similarly to the Texians or so mutilated when killed inside the fortress that they could not be identified as to proper allegiance. There is also the very real possibility that the official wanted to inflate and validate Santa Anna's victory claim a little. *El presidente* had already announced in writing that the number of slain enemy was 600.

This researcher in the archives that day, however, said, "Let me show you what I found a couple of weeks ago." He then turned some pages in the large book before him that contained numerous old documents carefully and protectively mounted inside. He turned to an official-looking old report with a double column of names within it.

"These are the names of all eligible voters who were in the Alamo in January 1836, sort of a voters' registration list for the time," he said. "It includes the names of several men who are not included on the modern rosters of dead. Between this and some other names I've found in letters and other records, I believe there really were 250 defenders who died there."

I was genuinely intrigued but too respectful of the man's work or afraid he would think I was trying to steal his research results or too shy to ask more questions. If he ever produced a book with his findings, I've not seen it, which means only that I've neither looked for it seriously nor bumped into it accidentally. However, considering how the "official" roster of the dead was compiled, he certainly may have been onto something.

There was no pre-battle list of men who were there, or at least none that survived and has shown up yet. A diarist named William Fairfax Gray recorded a list of 156 of the dead in March 1836, while the information was fresh and on everyone's mind, but some names appear twice, many are only a last name, and he described the names on his list as being only "as far as they are known." Other names were added in subsequent years, but ultimately it fell to the Daughters of the Republic, or ladies of similar ilk, to decide exactly who deserved to be included and who did not. One is tempted to speculate about these women sniffing and agreeing that so and so should not be included because, well, he just wasn't the right kind of people. Certain claimants, not speaking for themselves of course, were rejected for one reason or another. Point is, there might have been more than 189.

Returning to the present, the other critical piece of information needed for inclusion in my novel manuscript, which I called *Warnell's Souvenir,* was the identity or appearance of the flag that Warnell supposedly carried out of the fortress.

The flag of the Alamo might have been the tricolor with "1824" in its center, as depicted in various paintings of and movies about the Alamo but probably not. Such a flag existed and was even "adopted" in November 1835 by the provisional government of Texas as the "civil ensign and privateer flag." It was probably designed by a man named Phillip Dimmitt, and Dimmitt was at the Alamo, at least until the Mexican army showed up. He was a captain, in command of a small company of infantry, but when Santa Anna arrived unexpectedly on February 23, 1836, he and his lieutenant took off shortly thereafter, claiming later they were on some sort of important mission, the chief purpose of which was probably the preservation of their respective behinds.

The Dimmit flag signified support for the Federal Mexican Constitution of 1824, which encouraged immigration into Texas from the United States by awards of land. It was the legal incentive for most of Texas's first Anglican settlers, but in 1833, a new Federal Constitution was adopted that not only repealed the incentives to move to Texas but essentially outlawed immigration from the U.S. In response, many Texians began campaigning not for independence, but for re-adoption of the Constitution of 1824. Certainly there were Texians who championed that cause, particularly James Grant, who led an ill-fated expedition to take Matamoras in January 1836 and who pulled men out of the Alamo to do so. In fact, it is quite probable that the 1824 flag was flown when the Texians took the Alamo from General Cos in December 1835, but in all likelihood it was taken by Grant when he headed south, rather than being left behind for the remaining defenders to fly.

There is not only no historic record of that happening, but flying that flag would have been totally inconsistent with the sentiments of the majority of the defenders who stayed behind. Letters written by numerous men who were in the fort made it clear that their goal was independence, liberty, and establishment of a new nation, not a reversal of Mexican legislative policy. Instead, research suggests that a historian named Reuben M. Potter invented the story about the 1824 flag being flown, either to support the argument that the defenders were proponents of the Constitution of 1824 or because it was known that such a flag had, in fact, been adopted by the prerevolutionary Texas government. It can even be argued that many Alamo defenders would have been insulted, or outraged, if it was suggested that the cause they were willing to die for, and for which history would remember them, was reshaping of Mexican policy instead of total rejection of all Mexican authority.

What is documented is that there were at least three flags at the Alamo and possibly more.

The best known is the flag of the New Orleans Greys, which Santa Anna captured and which was carried back to Mexico as a trophy, mostly for the purpose of demonstrating that the citizens of the United States were aiding and fomenting rebellion in Texas. Despite various attempts over the years to bring it back to Texas, either by trading Mexican flags captured at San Jacinto or just as a gesture of neighborliness, the flag of the Greys remains in Mexico to this day.

Another documented flag was a Mexican tricolor with two stars, either gold or brown in color, set vertically in the center bar. Mexican staff officer and diarist Colonel Juan Almonte saw and wrote about the flag being flown in San Antonio as Santa Anna's army approached on February 23 and identified the stars as representing Texas and Coahuila. There is some evidence that the flag was flown by the militia commanded by James Bowie.

The third documented flag that was at the Alamo belonged to Lieutenant Colonel William Travis, but nobody knows what it looked like. The fact that it existed is based on Travis's diary, in which he recorded that on January 23, 1836, while en route to San Antonio, he paid five dollars for a flag.

Considering that Travis was initially co-commander of the fortress, with Bowie, and then its sole commander once Bowie became too ill, and considering Travis's egocentric personality, it seems almost axiomatic that the flag he would have ordered to be raised above the fort was one of his preferred design. Travis himself recorded that such a flag was flown when he wrote in his famous letter of February 24 to "the people of Texas and all Americans in the world," in which he stated that "our flag still waves proudly from the walls."

Perhaps, just perhaps, the flag that was flying was of Travis's design, and perhaps, just perhaps, it was emblazoned with the same words he used to close that letter: "Victory or Death."

The motto is certainly not historically unknown or unique. It—"Buaidh no Bas"—was the motto of both the MacDougall and MacNeil clans of Scotland and a variant of it, "Vince aut Morire" (Conquer or Die), was inscribed on the Bedford Flag, which was one of the first battle flags of the American Revolution.

It is also worth adding that one of the documented early flags of the Texas Revolution had similar words, "Liberty or Death," inscribed on one side. It was white with a blue star in the center and those words, also blue, beneath, and was made by Johanna Troutman, who is remembered as the "Betsy Ross of Texas."

She shouldn't be, because Betsy Ross was not a flag maker or at least not a maker of early U.S. flags, whereas Ms. Troutman definitely made this flag, of silk. She was the daughter of Hiram Baldwin Troutman of Knoxville, Georgia, and, when she heard that Colonel Fannin had appealed to that state for a company of Georgia volunteers to assist in the upcoming fight with Mexico, she made the flag and presented it to Captain William Ward and his company of volunteers in December 1835. It first flew in Velasco on January 8, 1836, over the American Hotel, after which Fannin took it with him to Goliad, where it was destroyed.

Travis was a pivotal figure in the disturbances at Anahuac, which is near Velasco, in 1835, but he was already on his way to San Antonio by the time the Troutman flag was hoisted. Still, there may have been a connection. Travis may even have suggested the design or heard about it from Fannin. It is also worth mentioning that the Troutman banner was the Alamo flag chosen for the IMAX film *Alamo: The Price of Freedom* as the one that was raised over the fort.

There were rumors of other flags flown by Texians at the Alamo, particularly one attributed to David Crockett and resembling the Star Spangled Banner but with a single large white star in its jack instead of multiple stars. Such a flag was authorized by Texas President David Burnet as the flag of the Texas Navy on April 9, 1836, a month after the Alamo fell. Finally, there were a few other flags flown briefly by some Texians during the last day of the battle, being white flags of surrender. Mexican diarist Enrique de la Pena noted that white flags hanging over the doors of some of the Texians' barracks, and other Mexican accounts mention defenders waving white socks on the ends of ramrods poked through windows or gun ports as fighting in the fort was drawing to its bloody finale.

Another Alamo fact I found interesting, which I've never seen discussed in other works about the Alamo and which I used in the work of fiction as a major key in the unraveling of the clues to the location of the flag in modern times, is the graffiti that has been scratched onto the real Alamo over the years since, and maybe even before, 1836.

One has to look closely, but when one does, it quickly becomes obvious that folks have been scratching names, initials, and comments on the walls of the old chapel, inside and out, for decades. For example, "NJD 1861" is carved to the right of one of the pillars next to the main entrance. Nearby, at hip level, is the date "1854." Past the doors is "Al" or perhaps "A.L." "Dounory." Lower is carved "J. Pool," "W.T. Tracy," and initials that are either "CTS" or "OIS." Near the statuary recesses are carved "M Kosse," "Martin Down," and "HAW 1861," along with something that looks like an Arabic "1" followed by either a question mark or an Arabic "2," followed by "o m." Inevitably there is the name "David Crockett" that we can be pretty certain was not put there by either simple old David or that Davy feller, as well as a nearby "J.B." that almost certainly does not stand for James Bonham. The word "WAR" is etched deeply into a stone in one of the recesses that once held a statue. There is a book in the making there for a patient and sharp-eyed researcher.

When Ann Richards was elected governor of Texas in 1990, the lady who was then serving as her general counsel in the Texas Treasury was Ann Schwartz. Ann had gone to law school with my wife, Patty, whom she called with an Alamo-related, more or less, proposition.

She knew that I had writing aspirations, and she had an idea for a screenplay she believed would be a winner. She also believed that she would follow her boss to the governor's office and that, once there, she would come into contact with various Hollywood types, who frequently show up to make movies in the Lone Star State. Her idea was for me to write the screenplay, her to get it sold, and for the two of us to divide the great fortune evenly. Needless to say, I agreed.

Her story idea was a darned good one, and neither Ann, Patty, nor I understood then or understand now why Hollywood has never seen fit to make it into a movie. It is the story of Emily Morgan or Emily West, "The Yellow Rose of Texas."

In a nutshell, Ms. West (or Morgan) was either a mulatto "indentured servant" or a free African American who came to Texas under a contract to work for a year. She was employed, according to legend, working at a plantation near the Texas coast when Santa Anna's army swept in, hot on the trail and the tail of Sam Houston's army. Emily was supposedly beautiful, and there is no doubt that Santa Anna had a thing for beautiful young ladies. He had "married" one during the siege of the Alamo, despite the fact that he already had a wife back in Mexico City, using a sergeant as a make-believe priest to perform the sham service, in order to dilly-dally with her under the guise of legitimacy and the girl's mama's approval.

In Emily's case, she was supposedly captured by the Mexican army and delivered to its commander who, legend has it, was quite willing to also be unfaithful to his fake Alamo wife in his tent the afternoon of April 21 when Houston attacked during siesta and won the war. When Santa Anna came out of his tent during the battle to see what all the ruckus was about, he was in his underwear.

The verifiable record is sparse but not nonexistent. Recent research indicates that the story is largely but not completely myth.[14] The popular version upon which I based my tale was that before being captured, she was known to be in the service of a landowner named Morgan and that the song "Yellow Rose of Texas" was written about her soon after the battle. "Yellow" is a synonym of the period for mulatto. "Rose" means beautiful woman. The last known record of Emily is that she was released and sailed, possibly back to New York City.

Pretty good yarn, methinks, and maybe the screenplay I wrote was okay too, but it is in the same dust bin with *Warnell's Souvenir*. To our mutual disappointment, Ann Schwartz did not follow the other Ann to the governor's mansion and never had the opportunity to peddle the manuscript.

That's about it for unpublished manuscripts about the Texas Revolution and the Alamo, except for one final, brief snapshot involving my daughter, Megan. She is a bright, beautiful young lady, but she has a very low tolerance for history, due largely to the fact that she has to endure so much exposure to it when hanging out with her mother, brother, and me.

When Megan was about five years old, we took the kids to the Alamo. As you know if you've been there, the inside of the chapel is a shrine. Gentlemen must remove their hats, and talking is expected to be kept to hushed tones. Inside are cases containing various priceless treasures and holy grails, including the ring Travis wore and gave to Angelina Dickinson—the "Babe of the Alamo"—who was the infant daughter of Susannah and Almeron Dickinson. The story goes that an evening or two before the Alamo was overrun, Travis picked Angelina up and lifted her onto his lap, took a hammered gold ring with a black cat's-eye stone off his finger, tied it through with a string, and slipped it over Angelina's head like a necklace. "If my boy was here," he supposedly said, "I'd give this to him. But I won't be needing it anymore, so you keep it for me."

My wife, Patty, our son, Nathan, and I were circulating respectfully through the display cases in the chapel, gazing at the holy relics, when Megan, who was decidedly not the Babe of the Alamo, marched up, tugged at my sleeve, and announced impatiently, "I've counted to one hundred and we're still here!"

It was time to move on. That's the way a lot of folks feel about history, which is necessary. Otherwise, we might never move forward.

Just Pretending, But Seriously

Those who cannot remember the past
are condemned to repeat it.
GEORGE SANTAYANA
"The Life of Reason" (1905–1906)

MY EXPERIENCE AT THE FILMING OF *NORTH/SOUTH II* IN 1986 LURED me into Civil War re-enacting the next year. I confess to having tried it once before, about 1975, along with some other J.E.B. Stuart wannabes from South Texas. While attending law school at the University of Houston I was invited to participate in a faux battle of Sabine Pass. I did so wearing what a private in an Army of Northern Virginia cavalry unit who idolized its commander might have worn, assuming said private had no horse, had located an 1860s source of polyester, and had zippers on his over-the-knee cavalry boots.

For anyone who might not know, zippers were not invented until 1893 and did not come into common usage until the 1930s. A Civil War re-enactor with zippers on his boots (or hip pockets on his pants, or belt loops, or wearing polyester) might just as well set himself on fire as expect to be taken seriously by dedicated re-enactors.

That 1975 experience provided me with exposure to some of the people who took re-enacting extremely seriously and convinced me there was a bright-line boundary to my passion for American history, beyond which lay landmine-strewn fields and strange travelers. I discovered, most particularly, that one of the "commanders" of the South Texas re-enactors was also a wizard, grand or otherwise, in the Ku Klux Klan. While my personal fascination with American history was intense, my disgust for white supremacists or racial bigots of any kind was just as intense, probably more so. Most of the serious re-enactors I met in 1975 were merely grown men who enjoyed dressing up and pretending to be Civil War soldiers, as I had done when a child. I'm all in favor of staying young at heart but not in the company of even one grown man whose heart is also saturated with racial hate. Loving the history of the South and simultaneously despising that aspect of its heritage is not a burden I bear alone.

However, discovering Professor Charles Sullivan and a few others in the hobby who not only shared my love of history but also had a sense of humor and enlightened political views improved my impression of re-enactors. In addition, the 125th anniversary of the war kicked off in 1987, right on the heels of *North/South II,* with gi-normous re-enactments of major battles scheduled.[15] I decided to participate in at least one and see what it was like. At the invitation of the leader of a Confederate infantry unit that attended the Freestone County Sesquicentennial Pageant, the members of which lived in and near Waco, I "enlisted" in the 7th Texas Infantry as a private. It, in turn, soon consolidated with a larger group "commanded" by a man who lived in Galveston, in preparation for participation in the re-enactment of the Battle of First Manassas, scheduled for July 1987 in Virginia.

Arguably, Civil War re-enacting dates back to the war itself, or to shortly thereafter. On at least two occasions, Confederate infantry brigades engaged in massive snowball fights with each other while in winter quarters, complete with battle lines, flanking movements, commanding officers, breastworks, and frontal assaults. In addition, a South Carolina Confederate veteran named Berry Greenwood Benson included in his 1880 memoirs a statement that is often cited by re-enactors as justification for their existence and that was read aloud by Shelby Foote near the end of the Ken Burns documentary about the Civil War:

Who knows but it may be given to us, after this life, to meet again in the old quarters, to play chess and draughts, to get up soon to answer the morning roll call, to fall in at the tap of the drum for drill and dress parade, and again to hastily don our war gear while the monotonous patterns of the long roll summons to battle? Who knows but again the old flags, ragged and torn, snapping in the wind, may face each other and flutter, pursuing and pursued, while the cries of victory fill a summer day? And after the battle, the wounded and slain will arise and all will meet together under the two flags, all sound and well and there will be talking and laughter; and cheers, and all will say, "Did it not seem real? Was it not as in the old days?"

Veterans and the U.S. Army conducted a few mini-versions of various battles on quinquennial and decennial-based anniversaries of the same, and some fairly large affairs accompanied the centennial of the war. The fact that some of those doing the faux fighting in the latter four years were firing blanks from M-1 Garand carbines and pump shotguns while wearing U.S. postal uniforms did not significantly diminish the events' popularity.

In the ensuing twenty-five years, the hobby matured—or at least those immature enough to pursue it found a lot of soul mates. Re-enactment units formed in virtually every state in the nation, notwithstanding that there had been no Civil War battles to re-enact in some or that the war preceded the existence of others. Significant re-enactment units were even founded in Europe, Canada, and Australia.

Again, I will leave it to other books—*Confederates in the Attic,* perhaps—to analyze America's interest in the hobby of re-enacting and will stick to telling about my own experiences, with only two more broad generalities about the re-enactors with whom I became acquainted.

First, while re-enacting seemed to attract all kinds, it included two distinct categories of folks who occupied opposite ends of a spectrum and who were destined to trash each other at every opportunity. One consisted of hobbyists who loved Civil War history, enjoyed pretending to be a part of it, and wanted the hobby to be a family affair filled with laughter, songs around campfires, women in hoop skirts, frolicking children, and ice chests of beer disguised as hardtack boxes in a tent. Unfortunately, this faction was often tolerant of less-than-authentic uniforms and impressions, a.k.a "farbiness."

At the other end of the spectrum were folks often called "thread counters." They wanted the re-enacting experience to be totally accurate and as authentic as humanly possible. Many had little or no tolerance for frivolity, costuming, or Hollywoodish behavior or may have been congenitally devoid of a sense of humor. Some were so determined to be correct that mere accurate appearance was not enough—buttons were required to have proper back marks and cloth could contain only the number of threads per square inch that was common in 1861–1865. I fell somewhere in the middle but decidedly closer to the former camp than the latter.

Second, a common goal of almost all re-enactors was to experience "magic moments." Sometimes these were mere seconds but a point in time when fantasy and scholarship intersected with reality and the present to produce a scene, sound, or sensation that was, at least to the one experiencing it, exactly as it must have been like in 1861–1865. I had a few such moments, and they remain in my mind today, as Charlie Sullivan used to say, as a mayfly caught in amber.

For First Manassas, the members of the unit I had joined actually boarded a train that carried most of them, although not me, from Texas to Manassas, Virginia. There they disembarked, and I caught up with them via plane and automobile, to march to the battlefield. We were about 300 strong and were portraying a brigade of Louisianans. We were accompanied by a full military band whose members marched and played to orders shouted in French and who affected the Cajun accents and attitudes they had either researched or imagined for the originals they were portraying. We wore natty cadet gray uniforms with white gaiters and white havelocks (cloth cap covers that hung over the wearers' necks as protection from the sun). We did look fine.

The march from Manassas station to the site of the re-enactment was about eight miles, and we made it in columns of fours beneath a broiling July sun, with the band playing "Dixie," "La Marseillaise," and other period tunes. Sweat ran off us in rivulets, baptizing the Virginia thoroughfares in an authentic fashion. When we arrived at the Confederate campsite, which was already populated by tens of thousands of spectators and other re-enactors, the band broke into "Bonnie Blue Flag," we came to the step, and a throng of people surged out to welcome us with cheers and shouts of admiration. It wasn't a magic moment, but it was definitely a vanity parade.

The ground was exceedingly hard to sleep on and the heat nearly unbearable in our wool uniforms, but the event went well. I experienced my first magic moment just before the "battle" began. We were marching up the back slope of what was supposed to be Henry Hill on a dirt road bordered by zigzagging split, or snake, rail fences. Near the top of the hill, a white frame house had been constructed to resemble the Henry house. Artillery was firing ahead of us, and pyrotechnic air bursts were going off at intervals overhead. We were just about to top the rise, when a murmur ran down the ranks, and the re-enactors ahead of me in the column began looking to their right and rear, some pointing.

I looked and saw a horse lying on its side some fifty yards away, its rider pinned beneath. Re-enactors were rushing to the aid of the man, who turned out to be our unit's lieutenant colonel. His horse had fallen and, we learned later, broken its rider's hip when it did so. Just then we topped the crest of the hill and saw the battlefield spread out before us. Three or four thousand men in regiments of Confederate infantry dressed in a variety of uniforms, colors, hues, and facings—blue, gray, white, yellow, and red—stood in battle lines or columns behind batteries of artillery whose gunners were working and firing their cannons. Stands of the first national banner, or Stars and Bars, and southern state flags snapped in the wind in a dozen places. Buglers, drummers, and fifers were providing a background score. Couriers galloped about the field on horseback. In the distance we could see a similar "army" drawn up beneath snapping stands of the Stars and Stripes and northern state flags. The time machine jolt of the dual sights of the fallen rider and the panorama of battle lasted less than a minute, but I'll carry it to my grave.

We fought the fight and won the day, after which I drove my rental car to Lexington to pay my respects to Jackson and Lee, who are buried there, and to spend a night with my cousins who live near my ancestral home. Then I returned to Texas. A good time was had by all.

The next big battle on the 125th's calendar was to be Shiloh in April 1988. Before that, the unit of Texas re-enactors I had joined was scheduled to participate in the filming of an IMAX movie to be called *Alamo: The Price of Freedom*, about that non–Civil War battle. The epic film was being made to be shown in San Antonio at a theater near the site of the real Alamo. It still plays there today and is well worth the price of admission.

Soon thereafter I managed to get elected second sergeant of the unit and volunteered to edit and produce a monthly newsletter. My wife, Patty, observed that I seemed to be getting serious about this new diversion rather than wanting only to experience a single big battle, and she was concerned. She'd been patient up to then, while minding her own law practice and raising our children, aged two and four. Now she decided she needed to take action in her own defense. Another wife might have laid down restrictions or informed me that my days of deserting her to pretend to refight the Civil War were at an end. A few wives might have expressed a desire to participate, all hoop-skirted and Scarlet O'Hara–like. Patty announced that if I was going to do this thing then so was she, and she intended to join the Confederate army and fight as a soldier.

I loved the sentiment. Her passion for history in general and the Civil War in particular were among the first things that attracted me to her, but I knew she was asking a lot. Whether weekend hobbyists or thread counters, most re-enactors drew the line at women portraying soldiers. As Mammy observed in *GWTW*, it "ain't fittin', ain't fittin', it just ain't fittin'."

Patty, on the other hand, was not going to be dissuaded by mere sexism. She'd been battling that sort of ignorance all her life. Her mother had been the first female pediatrician in Arlington, Texas, in the 1950s. Patty was a soccer-playing and -coaching, horse-showing, -riding and -training, tennis coaching and professionally playing, fencing instructing, independent-type lawyer. She knew she was as good as the next man and better than 90 percent of them. I certainly wasn't going to try to talk her out of trying to be as good a pretend soldier as any of them.

I began asking around within the Texas re-enactment unit to gauge potential reactions to Patty's proposal. Its captain, a handsome young auctioneer named Scott, and I had become friends, and he was not shocked by the prospect. Actually, he was too concerned about promotion up the line of command to worry about the plumbing of one of the rank-and-file soldiers. The Galveston colonel was about to appoint himself general, meaning the broken-hipped second in command and the unit's major would probably be promoted and there would be a major's slot available for Scott. He told me that if that happened he would support my succeeding him as captain. I was flattered by this but told him that my proposing nepotistic gender disguise might be considered by some of the troops as a loose plank in my platform. Scott acknowledged the problem but did not seem worried and did not tell me to forget Patty's joining the unit, my trying to become an officer, or both.

As a compromise and because participation in the filming of the upcoming Alamo movie was more of a movie-making pursuit than straight re-enacting, I sort of unilaterally arranged for her to join us for the last weekend of the scheduled ten days of filming. She had already been making preparations, trying out false beards and moustaches, seeing what it was like to wrap her chest tightly in an Ace bandage, and finding uniforms that fit. She already wore her hair short, and the impression she put together was quite convincing. I thought that perhaps if the other re-enactors saw that she was serious about discernible authenticity, they might overlook the indiscernible part.

The filming of the Alamo movie was a hoot. Each of us prepared by putting together a kit of a flintlock musket and its accessories, plus circa-1836-style Texian clothes, the pants, shoes, and shirts of which could be combined with the movie company–furnished jacket and shako, or tall military hat, of a Mexican *soldado*. Prior to the actual filming, however, word went out that the movie company was going to audition for the roles of the major historical characters of Travis, Crockett, Bowie, and Bonham. Scott decided to try out for Travis and did not have to twist my arm at all to convince me to try out for Bowie.

I shaved my moustache and grew an exceptionally repugnant set of long mutton chops, sideburns similar, sort of, to Bowie's. Scott, who supposedly had already been identified by the powers that be as their choice for Travis, was smuggled a contraband copy of the script for the movie, and he shared it with me. The word was that the audition would consist of our being handed a script, supposedly for the first time, and we would be asked to read and act out a particular scene. Scott and I were not averse to making full and appreciative use of our contraband cheat sheet. We were at war, after all.

In hindsight, the audition was so embarrassing I don't like to recall it, let alone tell the world about it, but a big part of trashing history is trashing my own earlier self, so here goes.

We journeyed to San Antonio on the big day and gathered, in full 1836 regalia, at a downtown hotel. The lobby was awash in Crockett, Bowie, and Travis characters, some wearing incredibly detailed costumes. My son Nathan, who was four and a half but already engaged in the adventure, came along, and when I took him into the hotel restroom, he spotted at a urinal another Bowie wannabe who was larger than me, and shouted, "Look, Daddy, there's another Jim Bowie. A fat one!"

The day of the audition just happened to be the same as my birthday, and I decided that getting a role in a historical movie might be just the present I wished for most. I figured Scott was a shoo-in, and I'd had a little bit of community theater acting experience, so I was cautiously optimistic.

The procedure was as we were told it would be. We were gathered in a large room, told the rules, and then asked one by one to read a scene from the script. The casting director and a couple of assistants served as *American Idol*–style judges. Scott did his thing, which was not quite as polished as I'd expected of him, and when it was my turn I was told to read a sort of lackluster set of Bowie lines. I did and was told "thank you." I knew I had not made an impression and that something more was needed so rather than step off the platform, I asked the casting director if I could read a different set of lines. He shrugged and said okay.

There was a scene in the script in which the terminally ill Bowie relinquished his command to Travis, telling his men, amid dramatic coughs and gasps, to follow their new leader as they had followed him. It was definitely Bowie's big scene and obviously the one most tailor-made for hamming it up. Nobody seemed to wonder how I knew the lines were there.

I coughed and gasped eloquently through the scene, and the room fell silent for a couple of seconds when I finished. Then the casting director said "I see from your application that today is your birthday, Mr. Akers." I nodded agreement, and he turned to the audience of actors and re-enactors and said, "Let's all sing 'Happy Birthday' to him!" which they all did, with the casting director loudly inserting "dear Jim Bowie" in the appropriate spot.

I had the role! I was going to be a star! I left the room and paced excitedly up and down the halls of the hotel. I was going to play Jim Bowie in a movie! Patty and Nathan were thrilled to hear the great news!

Har de har har. Neither Scott nor I got so much as a rejection letter. Real actors, Screen Actors Guild types, were chosen for the roles, including Don Swayze, the brother of Patrick, as Bonham and Merrill Connally, the brother of former Texas governor John Connally, as David Crockett.

The filming of the movie, however, was chock-full of adventure, startling scenes, and magic moments. It was made at Alamo Village, near Brackettville, Texas, which was first constructed for John Wayne's 1960 epic and which included full-scale versions of not only the entire Alamo fortress compound but a significant portion of San Antonio de Bexar and La Villita as well. After that movie was finished, the complex was retained as a movie set for other films, such as *Thirteen Days of Glory* and James Michener's miniseries, *Texas,* as well as a tourist attraction, which it still is today.

We lived, ate, and slept in the fortress for nine days with no modern conveniences. We filmed some days and all nights because the climax of the battle occurred in the early, predawn hours of March 6, 1836. Patty showed up on Friday evening and participated in the final two days of filming, passing completely undetected, except by those in my re-enacting unit who knew the truth and eyed her with suspicion.

Almost all of our camera time was as Mexican soldiers. We were drilled in Spanish in the School of the Soldier, a military instruction manual for the period, and had our faces and hair darkened if we were, as most of us were, white guys. I got to dress up and pretend to be a Texian three or four times, and the last time, during the filming of the final breaching of the walls, overrunning of the defenders, and subsequent massacre, I experienced a memorable magic moment.

The actual Alamo compound covered about two acres in addition to the famous chapel, and the Texian defenders constructed internal breastworks at the entrances to the barracks and other structures located inside the walls. These barricades were made of two rows of four fence posts set parallel to each other, around which cowhides where stretched, which were then filled with soil. Eight or ten of these, each about four feet high, two feet thick, and six or seven feet wide, had been constructed for the movie and placed in front of doorways inside the fortress. In the last scene filmed, in which I was allowed to be a Texian defender, I took position behind one.

The filming of each scene lasted four minutes, and when that one began the night was dark, but fires were burning brightly in various parts of the fort. Shells were exploding, there was a constant din of musketry, smoke was drifting skyward, and all cameras and modern facilities were behind us or out of sight. The north wall, considered to be the wall first breached by the Mexican attackers, was to my right, and I was on the equivalent of the east side of the plaza and parade ground with my back to soldiers' barracks that were once used as the mission's granary in the real compound. The Alamo Village version of the fort is not correctly positioned in direction, so that the historical north wall is actually, I believe, on its south side. Being bearings-challenged myself, this little discrepancy was not a problem for me. I have no idea how the thread counters managed to endure it.

I stood waiting, flintlock musket resting on top of the rawhide breastwork, as more and more blue-coated, white-pantalooned soldiers in black shakos began trotting into the interior of the fort. It was a forlorn feeling. There were other Texians not far away, but I was essentially alone and about to experience an inevitable faux fate. I could not only imagine but sense the despair the real Alamo defenders felt. There was no glorious future being purchased by my death, no sense of noble sacrifice for liberty—just lonely loss borne of backing the wrong horse. The magic of the moment was black, almost evil.

When the leading *soldado* was about twenty-five yards away, I fired at him. My nonexistent musket ball apparently missed, for instead of falling he stopped, leveled his rifle at me and fired back. I was partially exposed, reloading, and rather than prolong the inevitable, I let his shot kill me. He ran on, and I died a lonely fake death. It did not show up in the movie, of course.

Alamo re-enactors proved, if it is possible, to be more anal about historical accuracy and authenticity than Civil War re-enactors. There was a shorter span of time and fewer characters for them to focus their keen intellects on, and they did not welcome an intrusion from anybody who was merely a historical enthusiast. One day while riding into town with a handful of them, one of whom was the Jim Bowie wannabe whom Nathan had spotted in the restroom, I made the mistake of opining that maybe, considering that Jim Bowie's brother was named Rezin, pronounced "rosin," and because the song "Resin the Bow" was popular during the general time period of his birth, that the family might have named him after the song, which meant they pronounced their last name "Bow-ey" instead of "Boo-ey." The cacophony of hooting and cawing this suggestion set off made me thankful to escape with my life. Bow-ey indeed!

When the film was released several months later, Patty and I beat a path to San Antone to see it. We were not disappointed, except in the department of seeing ourselves on film. As with *North/South II,* I showed up only once, despite three or four instances of having been up close and full frontal to a whirring camera. That single appearance was in the far distance, standing on the wall above the main, historical southern gate, about a half inch high on a giant IMAX screen for all of two seconds as James Bonham, in the forefront of the scene, galloped toward the fortress on horseback. Patty, in a pattern that would repeat itself, showed up longer and larger, running across the screen as a Mexican soldier, although one has to be told it is she to know so. My only redeeming claim was that my miniscule appearance was in the guise of a Texian defender.

The Price of Freedom did not cause my Texas re-enacting unit to spread its collective arms in welcome to Patty. Just the opposite. While Patty and I researched and came up with a half dozen or so detailed accounts, out of what is believed to be 400 or so, of women who disguised themselves as men and fought in the Civil War, the other members of the unit began to hunker down behind philosophical breastworks. Texans are not exactly renowned for their liberal, open-minded points of view, and Texans who enjoy dressing up and pretending to be slave-owning Confederates are just a tad further to the political right than most.

However, rather than forcing the issue and bringing it to a head by petitioning that she be allowed to join the unit for Shiloh, I decided to make some phone calls and see if I could find any other re-enacting unit that would allow a woman in its ranks. After a few such calls I was directed to Charles Hillsman, who lived in Virginia and was colonel of a large unit that portrayed Longstreet's Corps. Charles, or Chuck, would later grace the cover of the August 15, 1988, issue of *U.S. News & World Report*, wearing his Confederate uniform as a prime example of the sort of folk involved in the re-enacting hobby. The previous month Gettysburg was re-enacted in what became the largest battle re-enactment in history, and few people deserve to be honored or used as a symbol of the hobby as much as Chuck Hillsman.

I didn't know until much later that Chuck had grown up surrounded and immersed in the Confederacy and the Civil War. His family previously owned the Hillsman house, which was at the epicenter of the Battle of Saylors Creek and is the focal point of the battlefield park today. From that house, Chuck's great-grandfather, James Overton Moses Hillsman, left to serve in the Confederate army as a captain under Stonewall Jackson. Wounded three times, he was captured at the Battle of Spotsylvania in May

1864 and was held prisoner until the end of the war. He was one of the Immortal 600, Confederate officer prisoners of war confined in a stockade on Morris Island, near Charleston, South Carolina, and intentionally starved and placed in the line of fire of Confederate artillery shelling the Federal army.

The Federals did it as retaliation for what they believed was similar treatment of Yankee prisoners by Confederates in Charleston. In fact, a Charleston newspaper had simply and carelessly reported, while castigating the Federal army for bombarding the civilian-filled city, that the Federals were endangering the lives of their own men in the city who were prisoners of the Confederates. This was misinterpreted to say that Confederates were intentionally exposing Yankee prisoners to cannon fire, so the 600 southern officers were brutalized in retaliation, sometimes tied hand and foot and left where they might be and sometimes killed by friendly fire. It was the kind of treatment that tends to cultivate especially hard feelings in victims, as well as their families and descendants.

If Chuck ever felt any animosity, it did not show. He was the epitome of a southern gentleman who desired only to honor the memory of his forebears and who harbored no political or vengeful motivations.

Upon hearing that two or three women soldiers were in his corps of Virginia re-enactors but knowing nothing else about him, I found his phone number, called, and explained my situation. After briefly laying the groundwork, I told him that my wife really cared about Civil War history and really wanted to serve as a soldier at the upcoming re-enactment of Shiloh, to which he drawled, in finest Virginia-ese, "Wall if that is sawmpthin' she has awlwuhs want'd t'do, who am Ah to say otherwise?" He told us to find him early the morning of the first day of the re-enactment, so that he could "examine her impression." I thanked him, and we hung up.

When the day came, Patty and I managed to find the camp of Longstreet's Corps shortly after dawn and met with Colonel Hillsman near his headquarters, which was on the edge of a sea of white canvas tents. He looked Patty over, nodded his approval, and pointed to where some Confederate re-enactors were building fires and beginning to boil coffee. "Go over and fall in with those men," he told her, "the ones with the short sergeant by the fire." She headed off in the direction he'd indicated, and I went in another to do my Texas second-sergeant thing.

Charles "Chuck" Hillsman, colonel, who commanded "Longstreet's Corps" of re-enactors during the 125th anniversary of the Civil War. This photo appeared on the cover of the *U.S. News & World Report* magazine dated August 15, 1988. Reprinted by permission of John McGrail, John McGrail Photography.

However, unknown to either of us, she stopped one short sergeant by the fire too soon, not at the camp of a part of Longstreet's Corps but at that of Company D of the 27th Virginia Infantry, a part of the Stonewall Brigade, under the command of Colonel "Rusty" Todd. We did not know, could not know, that this unit, which called itself the "Millets," had recently had a bad experience with one or more women. I don't know the details, except that it did not involve a female who wanted to be a soldier. Instead it was something about a wife or girlfriend or more than one who asserted her, or their, point of view too forcefully at a Millet event or several events. Knowing them as I later would, it probably involved something like complaining about too much drinking, farting, or telling off-color stories. Whatever it was, it resulted in a company vote not to allow any more women in the unit, no way, no how, no time, no kidding.

So it was that once Patty, a.k.a. "Pat," settled in near the fire and after a few of the Millets studied her, some of them came to the conclusion that she might not be their kind of member, pun intended. They weren't exactly rude about it, however. Instead, one of the Millet wags ambled over and began a conversation that quickly included the question, "Are you a woman?"

"Not today," Pat replied.

He returned to his knot of Millet buddies and reported his reconnaissance. This caused another one, probably either "the Mayor" or "the Chief," to stroll over, hold out his tin cup to Pat, and say, "Would you get me a cup of coffee, honey?" Pat looked at him and calmly told him what he could do with his coffee cup.

I should interject here that Patty looked long and hard before finding and selecting a suitable fake moustache for her impression. It was of good, theatrical quality, affixed with spirit gum, and looked quite real, but it caused her to be nearly incapable of smiling. She looked like a guy but a serious, unemotional sort of guy, for the duration of every re-enactment in which she participated. I suspect her unemotional but straightforward response that morning at Shiloh was regarded as just a tad intimidating or at least firm.

Patty, meanwhile, believed she was as welcome as rain and had the backing of the commander of the unit to prove it. She continued to sit near the fire, waiting for whatever was supposed to happen to start happening. Both at the Alamo movie and at home she had learned the basics of the School of the Soldier—facing movements and the manual of arms—so she had no cause to worry about being an awkward recruit and harbored no suspicion that she was unwelcome. The other Millets, of which there were twenty-five or thirty, were up and circulating by then, doing what Millets do, which was to crack wise, make rude noises, and carry on. Despite her being a strange sort of stranger among them and although her presence was of concern to some of them, they acted in their normal, boisterous, humorous way, and were friendly. She could not help overhear and be amused by a lot of what she heard. An inner corps of Millets had huddled, however, and decided that somebody needed to report this development up the chain of command, so one of them headed for the tent of their commanding officer, Rusty Todd.

Rusty was a Virginian with a long, full beard, natural leadership qualities, and a strong physical resemblance to the actual Stonewall Jackson, whom he portrayed at numerous re-enactments. He and his brother, who was known as "The Chief," were two of the original founders of the unit, and it was easy to understand, once you got to know him, why he was quickly selected to command the Stonewall Brigade, which consisted of the 2nd, 4th, 5th, 27th and 33rd Virginia Infantry "regiments."

On that particular morning, Colonel Todd, like Colonel Hillsman, was preparing to do what commanders of brigades of re-enactors do just before huge battle re-enactments, but when one of his fellow Millets approached to advise him of the threat that had invaded their camp, Rusty put his commander-type responsibilities aside for a few minutes. In a most un-Stonewall but very Millet-like move, he fetched a flask of bourbon, walked down to where Pat was sitting, and struck up a casual conversation.

He offered her a wake-me-up slug of whiskey, which she accepted, and then asked her who she was and what was going on. She explained the situation, which was that she was where she thought she was supposed to be, among the members of Longstreet's Corps. He explained that no, in fact she was among the Millets of the Stonewall Brigade, told her where Longstreet's Corps was located in the adjacent camp, and offered to have someone escort her over there.

Chuck and Rusty were close friends, and he was happy to do the favor. Pat, however, had been amused by what she had heard and seen so far in the Millet camp that morning and said no, she preferred to just stay where she was. Rusty said that would be fine, retrieved his flask, and headed back toward his tent. A covey of Millets encircled him to find out what the hell was going on, and he explained very quickly and to the point, that, "I can't tell the difference, and if I can't, then it shouldn't matter to you."

So it was that Patty was allowed to fight the battle of Shiloh amongst the Millets, of the 27th Virginia of the Stonewall Brigade. That afternoon, when I was able to take a break from my oh-so-important Texas second sergeant responsibilities, the first thing she told me, after a summary of the foregoing, were some of the jokes, jibes, and skits she had observed during the day.

The Millets were an unusual collection of clowns, comedians, and serious historians, who, at least in my 20/20 hindsight, had exactly the correct, middle-of-the-spectrum attitude about Civil War re-enacting. They took authenticity seriously and tried always to project the correct physical image, but they were there to have fun and not to inflict their private political, scholarly, or social philosophies on others.

The unofficial ringleaders of the Millets were the Mayor and the Chief, the latter being Rusty's brother and the former being the Chief's best friend. They were, simply put, a pair of Civil War comedians. The name "Millets" had originated at a re-enactment at which the pair, in order to avoid enduring drill, snuck off to take a nap in a nearby grain field. Upon awakening, the Mayor took a stalk of seeds from a plant and stuck it in his cap band. As they were leaving they encountered the owner of the field. When he mentioned something about the Mayor's hat decoration, the Mayor replied that it was maize, to which the owner said "No, that's millet." For whatever reason, they decided that should be the name for the whole company, and it stuck.

As an example of their attitude, when each major unit of the Confederate army at Shiloh was presented, later in the day, with a historically correct and lovingly manufactured reproduction of a battle flag that actually flew at the battle, the Mayor and the Chief immediately latched onto the one presented to the Stonewall Brigade and burned holes in it with cigarettes as pretend bullet holes. They had also perfected and performed a satirical manual of arms that involved a lot of dropping of rifles and holding them in awkward, imaginary positions not radically unlike a few real but odd ways that Civil War soldiers carried their weapons, such as "support arms" and "right shoulder shift." The Chief proudly and fiercely refused ever to clean or fire his rifle, which was essentially a long, musket-shaped piece of rust.

They liked to "forage," as had real Civil War soldiers, which in their case meant wandering around the re-enactor camps and absconding with anything useful that wasn't nailed down. At Shiloh they relieved some unsuspecting sutler of about forty cheap tin cups which they spirited back to the 27th's camp—"Milletville"—and tried unsuccessfully to sell to their comrades, describing for their product an imaginary provenance and location of recovery dating back to April 1862.

Virtually every member of the 27th acquired a Millet nickname. Many were earned by doing, saying, or looking like something stupid. Some were simply descriptive. The drummer was "Sticks." A humorous, scholarly member who smoked small cigars was "Stogie." A stout member was "Bear" and his son was "Cub." One who liked to build fires and blow things up was "Nitro," an overweight one was "Jabba," one who had overturned his car in a wreck was "Flipper," and so forth.

Shortly after the flag presentation ceremony but before that day's battle, the entire Confederate division of four or five thousand re-enactors was required to form up and pose for a huge panoramic photo that took nearly an hour to pose and that was then offered for sale to anyone who wanted a copy. Finding themselves at the rear of the large gathering of regiments and brigades, the Millets first contented themselves with chanting, "Take the picture; take the picture," for awhile and then, deciding they couldn't possibly recognize themselves in the finished product, fixed bayonets, placed their hats on the tips of the blades and hoisted them high in the air. Today, in the four-foot-wide framed photo that hangs in a back room of our home, I can be located fairly close to the front of the division, at attention with a blue second-sergeant's marker flag affixed proudly to the bayonet of my Enfield rifle. Pat is somewhere way in the rear, beneath twenty-five or thirty elevated hats.

I got my taste of the Millets on Saturday night, after a day of fighting Yankees with great solemnity and Texan seriousness, when I joined a group of them seated around a fire in Milletville. The Mayor had been persuaded to share some of his stories with those present, liquor was flowing, the night was cool but pleasant, and while not a magic moment, or series of hours, the experience became quite memorable. The Mayor was a computer programmer, but he had previously been a policeman, and was a natural raconteur. He told or repeated to us three tales about experiences he had had as a cop on patrol, each of which deserve to be an episode in a television situation comedy. By the time he finished, my sides hurt from laughing, and I was wishing the members of the Texas unit were capable of displaying a fraction of the Millets' humor and camaraderie.

Overall the re-enactment of Shiloh went off as it was supposed to, except that the "general" of our Texas unit decided for himself that he and his men would be heroes during the Sunday portion of the fight by making a long sneak attack through some woods in order to "flank" the enemy and win the battle for the Confederacy. Never mind that it didn't happen that way. Never mind that the re-enactment wasn't scripted for that to happen. He simply decided that it would be personally glorious, and that he would be the envy of all involved if he pulled it off.

"The Millets" after surrendering at Appomattox in April 1990, at the conclusion of the major re-enactments of the 125th anniversary of the Civil War. From left to right: Rusty, unknown, unknown, Ork, Stogie, Tim, Nitro, unknown (with blanket roll), Flipper, Sticks (black hat), Quickstep, the Chief (kneeling), Slander, Snack (kneeling), Buckwheat, the Professor, Scampi (kneeling), Ducky (wearing glasses), Greg (face behind Ducky), Ramrod, Fudge, Pogo, Judge. Image owned by author.

Following his orders, our battalion of three or four hundred soldiers did not participate in the main part of the day's battle and was involved instead in making a tiresome, circuitous march none of us had expected or planned for, then standing in a patch of woods for a couple of hours while everyone else was blazing away at each other. Finally, just before the battle was supposed to end, we came barreling out of the woods on the left end of the Yankee line, getting in among their rear, intending to deliver killing volleys and spirited Rebel Yells to win the day.

What actually happened was that by the time we arrived, everyone else was worn out and intent on wrapping up the battle so they could go home. Nobody expected us, and instead of acting flanked, shocked, or crushed, the Yankees just sort of looked at us quizzically. We charged in among them, during which I fired my one and only rifle shot of the day. The Yankees watched as we ran around yelling and making loud empty threats. Then they began walking away to start packing their gear and automobiles. We got back into formation and marched back to our camp, thence to the parking lot and on home to Texas. Our general later boasted of how we'd caught everyone off guard and how they had been devastated and at his mercy. Mostly, it was just the members of his own battalion who felt that way.

Pat, on the other hand, had a fine time, not only being in the midst of all of the faux fighting but earning a Millet nickname in the process. While preparing to go into battle, the Millets, like all participants, were told they must remove the ramrods from their rifles. The fear was that some overzealous re-enactor would use the ramrod for its intended purpose and ram a blank cartridge down the muzzle-loader's barrel, only to forget to remove and return it to its groove, or channel, in the stock beneath the barrel. Then, when the blank charge of gunpowder was fired, the ramrod would be launched like an arrow toward and possibly into another re-enactor. Such things happened fairly often in the real war, so that even having a ramrod on the field during a re-enactment was a safety violation.

Hearing the order to leave ramrods behind, Pat asked another Millet, "Where are we supposed to put our ramrods?" The Chief overheard, thought that was hilarious in a gender-based way, and she became known, then and thereafter, as "Ramrod."

Before they left, the Millets told Patty/Pat/Ramrod she could join up with them at any future re-enactment and could even bring me if she were so inclined. They were not going to change their rule about no women, no time, no how, but Ramrod was now an official Millet, not a woman. Besides, Millets enjoyed breaking the rules, even their own.

If there remained any sexist paranoia among any of the Millets, it was not apparent, although perhaps there were some who figured that with her in Texas and them in Virginia, there was no cause for concern. However, over the next two or three years, to the joy of American Express and American Airlines, we would prove them very wrong.

8

The Politics of Pretending

Politics are almost as exciting as war, and quite as dangerous. In war
you can only be killed once, but in politics many times.
WINSTON CHURCHILL

BACK IN TEXAS, THE DAY OF RECKONING REGARDING PATTY/PAT/
Ramrod's acceptance into the Texas re-enactment unit loomed large. I
unabashedly used my position as editor of the battalion's newsletter as
a platform to campaign for Patty's acceptance, but the rest of the group
grew more silent and more distant. It didn't help her cause that another
woman notified the unit that she was also looking for a re-enactment outfit
that would allow her to "jine up" as a soldier. Whereas Patty was in good
physical shape and tried to simply blend in with the other re-enactors, this
woman was hefty, overbearing, and combative.

We learned about an unwritten "twenty-yard rule" in regard to cross-
dressing re-enactors, which was that if an observer couldn't tell a soldier
was a woman from twenty yards distance, her impression was considered
to be historically acceptable, at least in appearance. Acceptance of Patty
into the re-enactment unit would set a precedent applicable to this other

lady, however, who probably could not have passed an eighty-yard rule, and would leave them only with her size as grounds for rejection. Considering that there were several guys in the battalion that would not have been able to pass a twenty-yard rule for authenticity based on weight that might have been a tad awkward. Even Patty, at least for the sake of historical authenticity, didn't want the Texas re-enactors to be saddled with that kind of a dilemma.

The deck was definitely stacking against us. Either that or somebody was cunning enough to stack it by getting this other woman to weigh in, so to speak, which is possible but not likely.

The Texans had a weekend drill scheduled a few months after Shiloh, and Scott said he would allow Patty to participate, after which the unit would vote on whether to let her join. For some reason I was unable to attend the drill event during the day on Saturday but arrived that evening for the business meeting, at which her Texas re-enacting fate was to be decided. Perhaps we decided it would be best for me to be absent, so that Patty could single-handedly demonstrate whether she could blend in with the rest of the Confederates wannabes. Fact was, if a fellow was looking for a sort of short, squarish type of Rebel, with a neatly trimmed moustache, blue eyes, and a firm set to his jaw, he didn't have to look any further than Patty. I knew she would do well with or without me.

When I did arrive, about sunset, she told me that Scott had drilled the unit mercilessly during the day, marching them long and hard, double-timing, and ordering sophisticated maneuvers under School of the Battalion, or military instruction manual for units larger than a company, that were new to a lot of the members and that were obviously intended to make it as tough as possible for Patty, in the hope of causing her to drop out and reveal her inadequacy. What happened instead was that several of the men in the unit became totally confused and frustrated trying to perform the unfamiliar maneuvers and some even fell out of the ranks, exhausted, at various points along the way, but not Patty. She could have matched them step for step, I suspect, all day and into the night.

Had the group recognized her determination and stamina, they could have chosen to rally around her, develop a bond, and take pride in her dedication to historical accuracy, as did the Millets. Instead, they took a sort of two-a-days callisthenic approach to the question of Victorian cross-dressing, with no intention to accept her no matter whether she proved herself or not. All it proved was that they were no more gentlemen than was Patty.

The meeting was held, before which I passed out printed propaganda describing and depicting various authentic women soldiers who fought as men in the war. I was allowed to make what I considered to be a sincere but level-headed speech, after which my dear friend Scott took the floor to explain why it would simply be wrong, so wrong, to allow Patty in the unit.

A few others said the same thing in less-complimentary terms. The question was called, and they voted one member short of unanimous against allowing her to join. The lone abstention—I didn't cast a ballot—came from the guy who had originally agreed to bring his re-enactment unit to the Freestone County pageant and who later invited me to join the 7th Texas unit of re-enactors. Such a rebel.

We left in silence, feeling rather like victims of Civil Rights abuse or at least re-enacted abuse but not really so much hurt as amused. That these modern, grown men, who liked to dress up and pretend to be long-ago men serving as soldiers in a previous century, could not tolerate the thought of a modern woman dressing up and pretending to be a long-ago woman who dressed up and pretended to be a man serving as a soldier from a previous century was almost too ironic to bear, at least with a straight face. In the immortal words of Forest Gump, stupid is as stupid does. Besides, we still had the Millets to fall back on.

Even before the Texas unit united in its rejection of us (well, her and therefore me), Patty and I had flown to Virginia to participate in the re-enactment of the Battle of Cedar Mountain with the Millets.

Cedar Mountain was fought on August 9, 1862, in Culpepper County, Virginia, just prior to the Battle of Second Manassas, between Confederate forces commanded by Stonewall Jackson and Federals under the command of Nathanial P. Banks. Banks was a politician who obtained a general's commission and was a general failure. He had tangled with Stonewall previously, during the Shenandoah Valley Campaign, during which the Rebels captured so much of his supplies and ordnance that they dubbed him "Commissary" Banks. Later in the war he commanded a Federal army dispatched to invade Texas in what became known as the Red River Campaign. Intercepted before he reached the Lone Star state line by Confederates under Richard Taylor, son of former president Zachary Taylor, Banks was soundly whipped by an army a third the size of his and was sent skeedaddling back toward New Orleans. The Yankees never were able to get much of a toehold in Texas, which means there isn't much in the way of Texas Civil War battles for modern Texans to re-enact or battlefields in which to search for artifacts.

At Cedar Mountain Banks came as close as he or practically anyone ever came to whipping Old Stonewall. In the end he didn't, but at one point in the battle the Confederate line—actually the famous Stonewall Brigade itself—broke and was streaming back in retreat, only to be rallied personally by Jackson who, intending to draw his saber for perhaps the only time in the war, discovered that it was rusted tight in its scabbard. In his pragmatic way, Stonewall unfastened the scabbard from its leather supports and waved it and the sword over his head, then seized a battle flag and, shouting for his men to rally around him, restored order, after which he went on to win the day. It was not as decisive a win as most of his, but it was still a victory.

The re-enactment was one of only a few that was fought, or re-created, on the actual battlefield, in this case beneath the looming presence of Slaughter's, a.k.a. Cedar, Mountain. This gave it some extra aura, and a bona fide magic moment occurred for several us when, while the Stonewall Brigade rested in the shade just before the battle, we saw Rusty Todd, as Jackson, galloping by on horseback, with his staff trailing after him like a comet's tail. His impression was so perfect, with forage cap pulled low on his forehead, sorrel-colored gelding beneath him, and a dozen or so staff officers, couriers, and a flag bearer in his wake, we felt like we were seeing Old Blue Light resurrected.

There were some other interesting moments, including the actual marriage of Sticks, the Millet drummer, to his bride in Milletville, a night artillery duel on the mountain, my being just yards away from Rusty when he re-enacted the rusty-sword brigade rally, and, particularly, an early morning "tactical."

A tactical is what re-enactors call an unscripted battle or attempted battle that has nothing to do with a historic event. In other words, the opposing commanders are given the opportunity to maneuver their "armies" against each other and attempt to defeat the other without any constraints of what happened 125 years earlier.

This one occurred early Sunday morning, starting before dawn and occupying about two hours. A thick fog had settled on the battlefield so we could scarcely see each other three paces apart, and it remained that way for the entire exercise. As a result the two groups of opposing re-enactors simply marched around in the gloom, listening hard and hoping to bump into each other. The experience was surreal. Each of us knew that in our immediate vicinity were a thousand other soldiers of our own side, with an equal number of the enemy somewhere not far away. We could each hear the clanking of tin cups and canteens, the tramp of feet, the swishing of grass against ankles, hushed conversations, and occasional hoof beats of a horse trotting or galloping nearby, but all any of us could see were the three nearest people.

A few confused rifle shots were fired but the exercise ended officially when our brigade suddenly and unexpectedly found itself on the receiving end of several dozen Federal cannons mere feet from our front, in line, loaded and primed, looming out of the mist like metal dinosaurs but mercifully not being fired. Had their gunners decided to pull the lanyards at the sound of our approach, the proximity of the muzzle blasts, even for a cannon loaded only with gunpowder wrapped in tinfoil, could have been fatal.

The next big event on the Millets' schedule, although not on that of the Texans, was the Battle of Chancellorsville. Virginia, Maryland, the Carolinas, the deep South, New York, Pennsylvania, New England, Illinois, and Ohio contain more Civil War re-enactors than the Midwest, Southwest, and far western California and Oregon portions of the country. Whereas there was at least one extremely large re-enactment in each year of the four years of the 125th anniversary attended by every re-enactor who could manage to get there, several staged along the east coast and in the deep South were attended almost exclusively by eastern re-enactors, plus the two of us.[12] Cedar Mountain and Chancellorsville fell into the latter category.

We attended Chancellorsville in May 1989 as members of the Stonewall Brigade and the Millets. It was held on the grounds of Fort A. P. Hill, near Fredericksburg and Moss Neck. The site was well-groomed and impressive, fairly reeking of history. Part of Jackson's Corps had camped where the re-enactment was to be held during the winter of 1862–1863, and we were told that during preparation for the event the site of a collapsed original Confederate winters quarters hut was discovered. Apparently the one-room building had caved in with two of its occupants inside, who were killed, and rather than dig them out and re-bury them, their comrades simply let the ruined hut serve as their tomb.

Representatives of a video company called Classic Images, which filmed all of the major re-enactments of the 125th, asked Rusty to portray Stonewall for their film, which included a lengthy, scripted re-enactment of his accidental shooting and mortal wounding the night of May 2, 1863.

Mounted, Rusty and a staff of twelve or fifteen officers and couriers recreated the tragic event with aplomb. Chuck Hillsman, portraying one of the staff officers killed by the volley that wounded Stonewall, did a backward somersault off the rear of his horse for the camera when the shots were fired. Rusty's horse did a superior impression of Little Sorrel by panicking much as the original had, galloping into the woods with a pretend-wounded Rusty flailing about on its back, wondering whether cinematic fame was really more important than survival. A fine time was had by all.

A few months before the event, however, before Patty/Pat/Ramrod and I packed our muskets and boarded another jet plane for Virginia, we became mired in a new and different type of trash history adventure—re-enacting politics.

The 125th was huge for re-enactors. Not only were there sham battles nearly as large as the originals and hours of magic moments in the offering, but several folks who had previously only pissed away their fortunes on Civil War history discovered there was now money to be made. Sutlers, musicians, writers, photographers, artists, uniform makers, arms makers, black powder millers, video filmmakers, and numerous other types of folks were catering wares and services to a swelling market of people who participated in and attended the re-enactments.

Another, less-practiced means of attempting to make one's fortune from re-enacting and the 125th anniversary of the war was by organizing the re-enactments themselves. Somebody had to plan, organize, implement, coordinate, and clean up for each gargantuan undertaking. Those things didn't happen by accident, and there was no *Giant Civil War Re-enactments for Dummies* template available. Tens of thousands of people would attend a re-enactment held at a site in the general proximity of a famous battle but on land previously the domain, mostly, of cows, horses, sheep, rabbits, and squirrels. Before that took place, somebody had to assume the responsibility, hopefully with at least a tad of experience, ambition, and/or ability, and get the land leased, parking areas set aside, authentic and modern campsites established, Porta Potties rented, drinking and washing water tanked in, medical staff hired, police protection secured, battlefield constructed, vendors and contractors paid, and a thousand other details accomplished.

Each re-enactor, sutler, and vendor would be required to pay a fee to participate, and each spectator would pay an admission fee to observe, so there was plenty of profit potential to pursue. However, there was no organization with oversight, jurisdiction, or rules for the sponsorship of Civil War battle re-enactments. In addition to the profit potential, there was also a truckload of risk. An unforeseen occurrence like a rainstorm could wipe out an entire event. The wounding or death of a re-enactor or spectator could bring civil and maybe even criminal liability. Still, people who cared about doing it, such as local nonprofit and historical organizations, expressed a desire to see a re-enactment happen and were usually willing to purchase insurance coverage. Nevertheless, it was up to some enterprising entrepreneur to actually pull it off. The time and proximity for the event were obvious to everyone, but there was a considerable challenge for the right person, or group of people, to put together enough time, money, and resources to get it done right. Anyone could propose an event, even schedule it and advertise it as the "official" battle, but there had to be the right kind of entrepreneur at the right time and place with the right backing and the right plan to put together an event that would attract enough re-enactors and spectators to actually become the official event.

And visible on the immediate horizon was the biggest, most profit-potential, most Disney-esque of them all: Gettysburg 125.

Looking back on it now, I suspect that either Rusty and Stogie or, more likely the Chief, had the bright idea that they and a few other Millets were more capable than anyone else of putting together the official Gettysburg 125 and that they could make a small fortune as a result. This is partly supposition on my part. Nobody ever said that is exactly what led to what followed. Instead, what I can relate is that (1) Rusty and some others were largely responsible for planning and putting together Chancellorsville 125, which was quite successful and well-executed; (2) we began hearing that the married couple who was planning and putting together Gettysburg 125, whom I shall call the Smiths, did not have a good reputation among certain re-enactors, particularly the Millets; and (3) beginning about eight months before the actual re-enactment, Rusty and the Millets launched a campaign to be the sponsors of the *real* Gettysburg 125.

The result was that sometime toward the end of 1987, after Cedar Mountain and before the Spring Campaign of 1863/1988, a political/philosophical/propaganda struggle was waged to attract the one thing that would decide where Gettysburg 125 would be "fought" and who would be responsible for its being the official re-enactment: attracting the largest number of re-enactors.

Besides being expensive, time-consuming, and looked on as a complete waste of time by nine out of ten normal people, re-enacting also suffered from an overdose of petty politics. Like little boys competing to see who would captain a sandlot baseball team or who would be the acknowledged leader of a band of eight-year-old cowboys, many of the commanders of the various re-enactment units across the country could be incredibly petty and spiteful in their treatment of other re-enactment leaders and their units. The more re-enactors there might be in one place, the more likely there would also be leaders and units who absolutely despised and constantly talked trash about the other leaders and units.

That was certainly so in Texas, where a lot of the re-enactors with whom I had once been a comrade were beginning to air more and more dissatisfaction with the Galveston general who had led them at Manassas and Shiloh. Similarly, in Virginia, there was an almost visible schism between the largest group of Confederate re-enactors, the Army of Northern Virginia (ANV) and a confederacy of the Stonewall Brigade, Longstreet's Corps, and a few smaller units. Everyone was superficially civil to each other because everyone wanted the same result—a huge re-enactment filled with hours of magic moments—but that didn't mean they had to like each other. Looking back I think that a lot of them subconsciously viewed the re-enactments in almost sexual terms, with lots of young bulls and studs performing mating dances and displaying garish plumage to try to consummate the event. Stogie and the Chief, with help from the Mayor and a few others, had transfigured the newsletter of the 27th Virginia Infantry from a monthly gab sheet into sort of the *National Lampoon* of re-enactor newsletters. They called it the *Millet Press*, and, due largely to some careful research and creative writing by Stogie, plus some ribald humor and satire by the Chief and the Mayor, it was an entertaining, informative read. This became the Millets' platform for a campaign to divert attention from the Smith Gettysburg 125 that was already being planned and was underway and toward Millet Gettysburg.

Again, I don't know all the details and must insert speculation where I have no facts. What I saw is this: the Stonewall Brigade (SWB), joined by Longstreet's Corps and some other Virginia-based Confederate re-enactment groups, let it be known that they had no confidence in the Smiths and that they had an alternative site, coordinator, and plan. All they needed was for some other large re-enactment units to see their point, agree, and shift a large number of committed re-enactor units to their side and site, thereby tipping the boat from starboard to port and making the Millet version the official Gettysburg of the 125th. Where Patty and I entered the picture is that we were perceived as being able to provide a bridge from the SWB in Virginia to the Galveston general–based Texas unit, at least in the way of introductions.

Never mind that we'd recently been drummed out of Texas re-enacting due to our radical gender views. Never mind that the board of officials comprising the local powers-that-be for the Texans included the future legal counsel for the Aryan Nation, which hints at intransigence. Rusty and Stogie latched onto us as a means of meeting with and trying to convince the Texans to switch sides. We, in turn, were flattered by their confidence and agreed to do all we could.

So, after a flurry of phone calls and borderline pleading, we managed to set up a meeting between Rusty and Stogie and the Texas re-enactor representatives to discuss which Gettysburg Texas would invade. It is remotely possible that we could have possessed a wee bit of influence with the Texas group, despite our recent rejection. We were, after all, two lawyers in a hobby which, while including a full range of lifestyles and education levels, seemed to be governed by folks who regarded us as incapable of deciding what was best for ourselves. We had also taken a somewhat admirable philosophical stand on the women-in-the-ranks issue, bounced when we were tossed, and had quickly gained the confidence of none other than Stonewall Jackson reincarnated. We might have, with just the right mixture of common sense, eloquence, and flat-on-our-back/belly-to-the-sky, beta-dog begging, been able to get them to take Millet Gettysburg seriously. That isn't, of course, even close to what happened.

Rusty and Stogie flew to Dallas, Patty and I picked them up, and we drove to Houston. The meeting was held in the law offices of the aforesaid lawyer. There were four of us and about ten of them. The foundation of the Millet Gettysburg argument in the matter was Rusty and Stogie's familiarity with the Smiths. They had attended re-enactments the couple had sponsored, had bad experiences, and predicted their GB 125 would furnish more. Overlying this was the verbal commitment of both a large landowner near Gettysburg and a financial institution to make the event happen if enough re-enactors committed. It all sounded plausible.

Except, of course, that the Texans were as united in their plan to just say no to Millet Gettysburg as they had been to voting about Patty's enlistment. The meeting accomplished nothing except that the Texans came across, again, as mean-spirited and petty. The highlight of the day turned out to be driving back to Dallas via San Antonio, showing Rusty and Stogie the Alamo, and treating them to some real Tex-Mex at the Mi Tierra Restaurant.

I think that Rusty and Stogie flying to Texas from Virginia at their own expense was their Pickett's Charge of the battle they waged in support of Millet Gettysburg, and the meeting was its high-water mark. The result was no more successful for them than Pickett's effort was for the Confederacy, and thereafter the dance of the dueling Gettysburgs slowly petered out and ended. However, the experience led to another development that had personal significance, which was that Rusty asked me to serve as adjutant of the Stonewall Brigade for Gettysburg 125.

I suppose down deep I'm snobbish, but the prospect of being an officer, so long as I was going to dress up and play soldier anyway, had immense appeal. Officers' rank was usually reserved for long-time unit commanders and their immediate disciples or for comrades approved by vote of a re-enactment group. If everyone who wanted to be an officer got to be one, there might have been an army of generals and colonels leading two privates, one drum, and a flag into battle. As a newbie to the hobby, I expected to have no more chance of becoming an officer than a white rat does of curing cancer, despite our respective close proximities to the efforts. Getting to be an adjutant not only meant I could dress fancy and get saluted but that I wouldn't have to march in formation and drill. It was a heck of a deal.

The brigade had an adjutant, briefly, at Chancellorsville. He was a shy, bespectacled government clerk nicknamed Pogo who still lived with his mother and collected Star Wars action figures. His principal claim to fame was that Stogie and the Chief had created a monthly column about him in the *Millet Press*. The stories in the column were purest fantasy and satire, in which Pogo occupied various positions of secret influence over principal historic events of the war, à la Walter Mitty or *Flashman at the Charge*. Knowing the real Pogo, compared to the imaginary superhero, made the column all that more hilarious.

As adjutant, however, Pogo just did not exude the Henry Kyd Douglas dash that Rusty wanted. Instead, he showed up, sort of like Stonewall at Fredericksburg, in a dazzling neon officer's uniform so un-Millet-like that the Chief accused him of having stitched gold Austrian braid to his socks. It's probable he did just fine handling the reports and paperwork that are the normal functions of an adjutant, but the Millets generally agreed that their rebels-without-a-clue image and Stonewall Rusty's impression would be advanced in a more satisfying manner if they had a lawyer for an adjutant, especially one from far-off Texas with a ballsy, or brass ovaries–equipped, wife.

Thus it was that at Gettysburg 125 I found myself occupying the lofty elevation and rarefied air of a major's rank. With only Pogo's mediocre Chancellorsville precedent to go by, I had before me a virtual tabula rasa of role-playing to assume, and I did it with all the panache I could muster.

Despite dire predictions to the contrary, the Smiths did a superficially okay job, at least in the sense of pulling together an absolutely colossal event. There were more than 20,000 re-enactors present and probably 100,000 spectators over its three-day duration. Everything about it was impressive and as close to being the real thing as can be had short of being a real thing. Magic moments were easy to come by, and although the coordinators failed in several significant ways, particularly including not getting the fences that lined the re-created Emmitsburg Pike constructed, I doubt that most re-enactors or any of the spectators particularly noticed.

The Emmitsburg Pike fences were critical to devoted re-enactors and historians because they played a significant role in slowing down and breaking up Pickett's Charge on the third day of the actual battle. The real soldiers of the three Confederate divisions who made the attack were forced to stop, or at least pause, when they came to the two parallel fences on each side of the turnpike. They had to either climb over or tear down the obstacles, which not only slowed their momentum but allowed the Federal defenders to mow them down efficiently and effectively. Pickett's Charge was a grand assault before the attackers got to the fences, after which it became a disorganized mob. A few Confederate outfits stopped at the fences and went no farther.

For the re-enactment, however, the two rail fences consisted only of rails scattered on the ground that had never been turned into the fences that were promised and had no effect on the re-enactors' recreation of the famous charge. Still, except for this and some other matters, the Smiths not only got credit for a good event but continued in the business, ultimately contracting with Ron Maxwell to assist in the production of Michael Sharra's *Killer Angels*, which was released in 1993 as the movie *Gettysburg*, starring Martin Sheen, Tom Berringer, and Jeff Daniels. By then, however, the rest of the re-enacting world had discovered what Rusty et al. knew years before. An Internet site concerning the making of the movie mentions them as follows:

> This market in turn had been cornered by an enterprising couple named [Smith], whom Maxwell was now counting on to deliver for the new enterprise. Unfortunately, they had worn out their good standing among major re-enactor constituencies. . . . Having served out earlier hitches, they (re-enactors) now demanded re-enlistment bounty . . . with an additional bonus for each man over the minimum; an on-site historian acceptable to the negotiators would be engaged to insure historical "accuracy" and to take over "re-enactor coordination" activities from the despised [Smiths].[16]

As for my new job as adjutant, other than filling out daily forms for unit strength, drafting after-battle reports, and looking good in knee-high boots and my own gold trim, my most significant role was the accomplishment of dress parade.

Dress parade is not like what it sounds. It does not involve soldiers putting on their best uniforms and marching down a street. It was a daily, sometimes twice-daily static ceremonial formation at which troop strength was ascertained and orders from the commanding officer were delivered. It was essentially the only formation of common usage, at least by re-enactors, that was run by the adjutant. This is how it was conducted:

The battalion, normally a unit of soldiers larger than a company (forty to 100 men) but smaller than a regiment (400 to 1,000 men) would fall into line of battle at parade rest, meaning they would form up in two long parallel lines facing forward. Each captain or other company commander stood centered in front of his company in its place in the line. The commanding officer of the battalion stood centered in front of and facing them, with the color guard in the center of the first rank. All other officers and certain noncoms, such as first and second sergeants, had other traditional positions to occupy. On the far right end of the front rank would be whatever musical band the battalion possessed, often no more than one or two drummers and a fifer. The adjutant stood to their right. When the adjutant ascertained that everyone was in the proper position and perhaps after a suitable passage of time in which to get serious, he would draw his saber and shout "Battalion . . . attention," followed by "shoulder arms," followed by "to the rear in open order . . . march." At the latter command the rear rank would take four steps backward. This opened the two ranks to a width that would allow inspecting officers to move freely between the ranks if an optional inspection was to be included in the dress parade.

The adjutant would then bring them to order arms, would right face and shout "Musicians . . . beat off," and usually some wag in the ranks was ready with an off-color observation about what that order meant. Undeterred, the band would step forward out of the line, following the sotto voce commands of the chief musician, perform a left wheel, commence playing a martial air or at least a drum cadence, and march down the entire length of the front rank, counter march, and return the same distance, then wheel and about face into its original position.

The adjutant would then step forward, with his saber drawn and carried at shoulder arms, and march alone down the front rank until he was even with the commanding officer, at which point he would stop, right face, take a few steps forward, halt, salute the commander with his saber (i.e., raise it from his shoulder, turn the blade sideways with its right side facing the commander and lifted to a position with the hilt in front of his face and the base of the blade covering his right eye, then sweep the tip of the blade down in an arc ending with the tip just in front of his right boot toe). He would shout, "Sir, the parade is formed!" The commander would return the salute and would say "post," at which point the adjutant would march forward, pass on the commander's right side, then right face, step, right face, and stop, positioning himself two paces behind and one pace to the left of the commander.

The commander would then tell his troops whatever he wanted them to hear, after which the adjutant would march back out and, with his back to the commander, would shout, "First sergeants, front and center . . . march!"

Each first sergeant, being one per company, would then march forward from his position at the right end of the front rank of his company and, performing his own left or right face, would march to a center position facing the adjutant. When all were in their places but still facing in the direction they had marched, the adjutant would shout "front," and the NCOs would turn toward him. He would then shout "report," and each sergeant, in order of company, would shout out the strength of his company, such as "Company A, forty-three men present and accounted for, six in hospital, two unaccounted for," or whatever. As this was going on the adjutant would hurriedly scribble the numbers in a notebook, tally them, and when they had finished would about-face, salute, and shout the total battalion strength to the commander, who would return the salute. The adjutant would then about-face and command, "First sergeants, outward face," and they would turn whichever direction they needed to face to return to their companies. The adjutant would command them to march, and they would go back to their positions.

At this point the commander might take over, order ranks closed, and dismiss the parade or allow the adjutant to do so, unless he had instructed the adjutant, for example, to deliver particular additional orders for the day to the battalion or to particular companies or individuals.

I decided and convinced Rusty that this was the point at which I could jazz things up. Instead of Rusty delivering orders for the day when it was his turn to talk, prior to obtaining the sergeants' reports, he would, prior to the parade, tell me what orders he wanted delivered, and I would, preparatory to delivering them, shout, "Attention to orders!"

Then, before telling the members of the Stonewall Brigade what was in store for them for the day, I would deliver my own brand of Civil War re-enactor/magic moment, harangue about where we were, why we were there, what happened there 125 years previously, and what it all meant—sort of a personal "attention to ardors." It was cornball in the extreme, but the re-enactors loved it.

The re-enactment lasted three days, naturally, with one of the real conflict's three days of battle re-enacted each day, and the first time I pulled this off, which was either the evening of the day before the first day's fight or the morning of, it went marvelously.

I have no specific recollection of what I said, but it was a mixture of historical fact, honoring of those who went before us, pumping up of the re-enactors as though what they were doing had meaning, and a fair amount of poetic license. The members of the Stonewall Brigade ate it up like candy. I could actually see tears glistening in some eyes, and individual members came up afterward to tell me how much they enjoyed what I'd said. It was heady stuff in a daffy way and gave me license to make it even more heady.

So, each day, or sometimes twice, my harangue got better and better, if I do say so myself. The third day's parade, which was the last, preceded Pickett's Charge. It was the climax, both of the re-enactment and my flowery speechifying. I recall that I asked in a dramatic, rhetorical fashion why the charge was made, pointing out that General Lee was quite familiar with the results of charging uphill toward an entrenched enemy, à la Malvern Hill and Fredericksburg. Then I built on the premise of it shouldn't have happened, speculating about what might have occurred had the charge not been made and an alternative, successive maneuver been executed, building in passion to a loud, pleading, or bleating, of "Why? Why? Oh, why?"

My dénouement was an almost prayerful benediction, verbally saluting the flower of the South who tried so valiantly that day and died in the process but winding up with a sincere expression of appreciation that it didn't happen any other way except the way it actually did in light of the way things turned out, the marvelous nation we were all a part of in modern times, the fact we'd all gotten born, and so forth. The sap fairly oozed from my lips, and more than one man covered his face with a hand and wept openly. Goodo.

My brother-in-law, Patty's brother, who is a computer programmer with no particular interest in history, had accompanied us to Gettysburg 125 to see what being in a battle re-enactment was like. He was in the ranks as a private, listening to me that day, and he's never been comfortable around me since. I'd proved to be way too weird to be a trustworthy member of the family.

My other nerdish accomplishment of note was the drafting of authentic-sounding after-battle reports about the involvement of the brigade in each day's scenario. These were delivered the evenings of the first and second days at the headquarters of the re-enactor general commanding the Confederate army. There was a Robert E. Lee look-alike in attendance at the re-enactment, but he was just for show and the spectators. The actual army commander was a long-bearded, courtly gentleman who occupied the re-enactor position of commander of the ANV.

All of the major battalion and brigade commanders on the Confederate side attended these post-battle scenarios, including our old friend, the general from Galveston, as well as Chuck Hillsman and other luminaries of the re-enactment life. Although Chuck had just appeared on the cover of *U.S. News & World Report*, his Longstreet's Corps and Rusty's Stonewall Brigade had, as punishment for waging the dueling Gettysburgs campaign, been relegated to rear rank, sucking-hind-titty positions in the scripted battle events, while the Texans and the other Tories were assigned the choice roles. Those battle reports the two evenings at army headquarters, however, helped untarnish Rusty a bit and nearly made him shine.

The adjutant of each of the five or six different battalions delivered an after-battle report to the commanding general and his staff, and most of them had invested little or no effort preparing for it. I, on the other hand, clutched and read from a two- or three-page missive constructed of Victorian language patterns and historical accuracy mixed with real-world recent events, delivered in my best courtroom diction. Rusty and Chuck fairly beamed as I did so, while General Galveston's expression of smug satisfaction eroded gradually into a resentful sneer.

The next big re-enactments on the 125th calendar were Chickamauga, Atlanta, Wilderness/Spotsylvania, and Saylors Creek/Appomattox. There were a few others, like The Crater and Bentonville, which we didn't attend, as well as Mansfield/Pleasant Hill in Louisiana, which is held annually and to which we did go, falling in with some unit of tolerant strangers. I was a full-fledged Millet by then, with the sobriquet "Judge," and I served for a couple or three years, with Stogie, as co-editor of the 27th's newsletter, which succeeded the *Millet Press* after it became temporarily defunct for reasons not worth describing.

A new and unexpected phenomena occurred between Gettysburg in July and Chickamauga in September, in the form of my being asked by the commander of another re-enactment unit to serve on his staff when he commanded the loose equivalent of the next step up in military unit designation, a division, within which the Stonewall Brigade would be included. In other words, I was asked to serve on the staff of Rusty's commander. This oddity was repeated for Atlanta and Wilderness/Spotsylvania, and I even received a similar invitation to serve under the general commanding the ANV at a post-125th event we were unable to attend.

I should have declined the invitations and adhered to a dance-with-the-one-who-brung-you form of loyalty to Rusty, but I was a re-enactor whore. I accepted the invitations, flattered, due in part because doing so elevated me in rank to lieutenant colonel and adjutant and inspector general status while still being part of the same, just larger, unit that included the Millets. I returned to Rusty and the Stonewall Brigade, however, for Saylors Creek and Appomattox, at which I stood beside Rusty as Lee's Miserables (a common nickname given the Army of Northern Virginia, based on Victor Hugo's 1862 novel), surrendered, wearing three stars of a full colonel. I was proud to have gone off to "war" at First Manassas as a private and to have come out four years later a colonel. Doing so was not comparable to or as glorious as certain genuine military accomplishments, like a weekend cleaning latrines at boot camp, but it is what it is and was what I had.

We also attended the Remembrance Day event held at Gettysburg each November, at which the Millets scheduled their annual banquet. The day began with a long parade for the tourists, then vanity prancing around the town in uniform, followed by an evening of dress uniforms, meal, speeches, and ballroom dancing (at which Pat/Ramrod was all Patty), followed by drunken revelry. Another favorite memorable incident occurred at one of the latter.

Thirty or so of us, Millets and significant others, had retired from the banquet room to a suite of rooms in the Gettysburg hotel in which the party had been held, where we proceeded to drink ourselves into oblivion and sing favorite Civil War songs. I was able to participate actively in both these pursuits, having a tolerant liver and having always loved the music and lyrics of the period. This latter inclination, in fact, had been one of the things Charlie Sullivan and I discovered we shared a love for during *North/South II*. He had subsequently mailed me tape cassettes of some of his favorite tunes, one of which was a World War I song about the battle of Gallipoli. The first-person lyricist/singer was an Australian who lost his legs in the battle, and it was truly a fine example of that sort of historic, militaristic, tear-jerker ballad.

Predictably, several Millets were also familiar with it, but while we were able to come up with some of the lyrics, we could not, to save our besotted souls, remember the tune. We thought and thought and sang and sang various close-but-no-cigar melodies, getting drunker and more determined as the night wore on. Finally, I announced I would solve the problem by calling Charlie Sullivan.

It was about 3:00 A.M. in Gettysburg, meaning it was 2:00 A.M. in Perkiston, Mississippi, but I had his number, found a phone with a speaker feature, and dialed. Charlie answered sleepily on the sixth or seventh ring.

I described our situation and the critical nature of the problem. Charlie listened without complaint, question, or argument, and when I finished, he paused a few seconds and then sang the song in a clear, welcome, confident baritone. The room erupted with Rebel Yells and applause.

In 1992, word came down that a movie was going to be made from the book *The Killer Angels* by Michael Sharra. This 1974 novel about the Battle of Gettysburg won a Pulitzer Prize in 1975 and is, along with *Company Aytch* by Sam Watkins, and *JEB Stuart* by John Thomason, among my favorite books about the Civil War. The movie company, headed by Ted Turner, was inviting or soliciting re-enactors to be in the filming, a portion of which would be on the actual battlefield. As evidenced by the quote about the Smiths, above, a lot of re-enactors were a little more hesitant to just jump in the movie bed for free than they had been for *North/South II*, *Glory*, and some others, but Patty/Pat/Ramrod and I could not be counted in that class of careful negotiators. We jumped at the chance, flew back East to participate, and were paid two ball caps and one T-shirt that had "Killer Angels" printed on it, fifty dollars in travel expenses, and later got our names put in a booklet mailed out to all participants.

I was on-site for only about four days, but Patty was able to stay three more, which resulted in her showing up in the movie, renamed *Gettysburg*, during the Little Round Top portion of the film. Before I left we were able to participate in some filming of the first day's battle and got to sit on the ground with a group of other re-enactors pretending to be soldiers of the 1st Maine Infantry listening to a speech from its commander, Joshua Chamberlain. He was portrayed by Jeff Daniels, and it was great fun to be close to him as the speech-making was filmed.

After I left, when Little Round Top was filmed, Patty/Pat/Ramrod not only wasn't identified as the total scoundrel she was, faking manhood, and not only showed up five or six times in the movie but was actually selected out of the ranks to be in a hand-to-hand combat scene with one of the movie actors, due to the fact that he was only a little taller than her five

Author Monte Akers, at right, and his wife, Patricia (Patty/Pat/Ramrod) Akers, during the filming of the movie *Gettysburg*. At far left background, mounted on a horse, is the actor C. Thomas Howell, who portrayed the brother of Colonel Joshua Chamberlain in the movie. Image owned by author.

feet four inches. That scene, however, along with all in which I may have appeared, wound up on the cutting room floor.

We spent nights on the movie battlefield, a portion of which served as a Confederate hospital site after the real battle, and some of the corps of hard-core re-enactors who had been there for the duration, including one we had met and made friends with during the filming of *Price of Freedom*, reported inexplicable tales of perceived hauntings. They included cold spots, unaccounted-for voices, and, in the case of our friend, having the blanket pulled from him as he was drifting off to sleep, although there was nobody present when he looked up to see who had done it. We observed a particular tree, probably a witness tree, in a field that frequently had its own cloud of fog or mist beneath its canopy in the evening, even though other trees did not.

Perhaps the most amusing circumstance worth repeating resulted from Patty's excellent impression of a soldier. We normally formed up and stayed with the same group, or unit, of extras during the filming, and the fellow

Half-plate ambrotype made in 1998 by Wendell Decker, using a camera of Civil War vintage, of the author and his family at the 135th anniversary re-enactment of the Battle of Gettysburg. Seated, Monte and Nathan; standing, Patty and Megan. Note that Megan's face is blurred because she moved slightly during the several seconds required to take a photograph of that period. Courtesy of Wendell Decker, Vintage Image Studios.

next to Patty never suspected that she was not what she appeared to be. There were, on the movie set, a half dozen or so young ladies, quite attractive, whose job it was to apply makeup—mostly fake dirt—to the re-enactors. On more than one occasion, this fellow would elbow Pat and direct her/his attention to one of these ladies and make a comment such as "Get a load of that one" or "Check out the rack on that one." Patty never revealed the nature of his misunderstanding to him.

We took a break from the hobby a year after the filming of *Gettysburg*, but by 1995 our son, Nathan, was approaching drummer-boy age, and he longed to participate, so we enrolled him in drum lessons, and he became a crackerjack drummer who participated in a dozen or so faux battles over the next few years. Once, at the annual Mansfield–Pleasant Hill re-enactment, he was the only Rebel drummer at the event and performed marvelously for the entire Confederate "army" of 500 or so soldiers.

Our beautiful daughter, Megan, who absolutely despises history, even succumbed to the seductive lure of hoop skirts and joined us for a couple of events. At several re-enactments one or more of us had our photos taken by "artists" using authentic ambrotype, tintype, or carte de visite cameras, and we have a small collection of such images with but not amongst, my artifact collection. My favorite is a half-plate ambro we had taken at Gettysburg in 1998, with me as a grizzled, gray-bearded officer, Nathan as a callow sixteen-year-old, Patty/Pat/Ramrod as a serious-looking rebel private, and Megan as a young Melanie Wilkes.

We haven't participated in a re-enactment for several years now and never will again. I've definitely outgrown the addiction in age, inclination, philosophy, and physical ability to look correct. I don't readily admit to folks who know me that I was ever seduced by such a strange, puerile pursuit, but the memories are warm and still make me smile.

9

Comanche, Custer, and a Con Man

They were right, tight boys, never sulky or slow,
A fruitful, a goodly muster.
The eldest died at the Alamo.
The youngest fell with Custer.
STEPHEN VINCENT BENÉT
"The Ballad of William Sycamore" (circa 1922)

WHEN I WAS IN TEN I ORDERED *COMANCHE OF THE SEVENTH,* BY Margaret Leighton, a book for juveniles published in 1957, from a monthly selection of paperbacks that students back then could acquire for about thirty-five cents each. It was the story of the bay gelding ridden by Captain Myles Keogh, who commanded Company I of the 7th Cavalry at the Battle of the Little Big Horn.

Although certainly not the only horse to survive the battle, Comanche was the only one that the regiment rescued from the battlefield and took back to Fort Abraham Lincoln to nurse back to health from the seven wounds it had received. Thereafter the animal became known as the only survivor of Custer's Last Stand, a claim that myopically ignored the 3,000 or so Indians and other horses who lived through the event.

The book did what the author intended and fueled fires in me. I cried when the horse died, broken-hearted at the loss of its second master, Gustav Korn, recently killed at Wounded Knee. I longed to hear the tune of "Garry Owen," the 7th Cavalry's anthem, and to figure out exactly what "lilting" meant, which is how Ms. Leighton described the song as it played in Comanche's death-stall imagination. I vowed to go see the horse, stuffed and on display at the University of Kansas in Lawrence, and finally got around to doing it at age fifty-eight. Shortly after I read the book, about age ten, Johnny Horton released the song "Comanche, the Brave Horse," about the same animal, and Walt Disney obligingly released *Tonka*, starring Sal Mineo, also about the horse. I was bitten by the Custer bug, then re-bitten, and infected, like millions, apparently, of other Americans.

The book is what did it, although I possessed a claim to interest in Custer that most others did not. My father owned a ranch, where I was reared, on the Oklahoma-Texas border only about forty miles from Cheyenne, Oklahoma, site of the Battle of the Washita. There, on November 27, 1868, Custer and his 7th Cavalry attacked a village of Southern Cheyenne Indians under a chief named Black Kettle, killed somewhere between thirteen and one hundred of them, including the chief and his wife, along with 850 Indian ponies, with a loss of twenty-one soldiers. The battle laid the groundwork, in ways no one then suspected, for Custer's own demise eight years later in Montana. It was also the battle depicted in the 1970 movie *Little Big Man*, starring Dustin Hoffman, in which Jack Crabb's lovely Cheyenne bride, Sunshine, and their infant son, were killed.

My father's ranch was located near the line of march followed by the 7th on its way to the battle from Fort (then Camp) Supply, near Woodward, Oklahoma. Even more personal was the fact that one of the most prominent points on the ranch was a long promontory called Musket Ridge. There, when the land was in the ownership of my uncle during the 1940s, a ranch hand found a rusted muzzle-loading rifle along the top of the ridge. Soon thereafter, probably at the invitation of my uncle, archaeologists from a nearby college located and exhumed the skeleton of an Indian from a shallow cave high on the face of the ridge, near where the musket was found.

I have practically no evidence to support it, but I like to think the dead Indian might have been mortally wounded at the Washita and buried on the ridge soon thereafter. I was able to confirm that this type of burial was consistent with the practices of the Southern Cheyenne, and the fact that

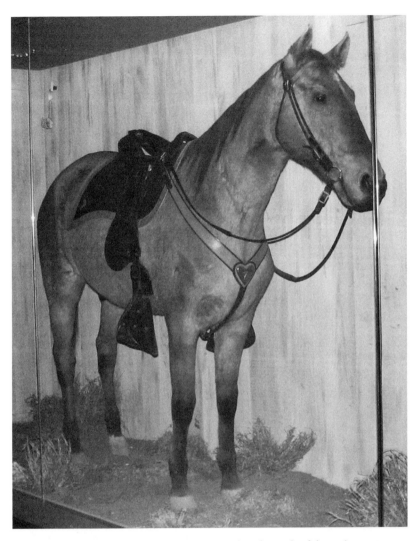

Comanche, the horse ridden by Captain Myles Keogh in the Battle of the Little Big Horn, remembered as "the only survivor" of Custer's Last Stand, preserved and on display at the campus of the University of Kansas in Lawrence. Song and legend record that Keogh and Comanche shared an exceptionally close bond, although the captain rode a horse named Paddy more frequently. Courtesy of University of Kansas Natural History Museum.

there was a musket buried with the Indian suggests that it was a warrior of the mid-1800s. And there is the geographical proximity, but I suspect the notion is just wishful thinking and more trash history.

Yet it was not the Battle of the Washita and its proximity to my home that got me interested in Custer and the Little Big Horn. To the contrary, half a century passed before I read any real detailed accounts of the 1868 battle and Custer's contemporary movements in the area. Then I learned, to my chagrin, that the 7th Cavalry frequently rode and camped along Wolf Creek and other childhood stomping grounds of mine and that Keogh and Comanche, while not at the Washita, were involved in another nearby Indian expedition led by a General Alfred Sully just prior to the Washita, in which Comanche was wounded by an arrow. Had I known that as a boy, I might have researched the stories exhaustively, ridden the same routes, relic-hunted the campsites, and generally been more of an irritating history nerd than I was.

I became interested in Custer's Last Stand for the same reason that millions of others became interested. No other battle in American history, it is written, has generated as many books and paintings, or as much controversy. Even though it was a small affair by Civil War and World War II standards, it occupies a titanic amount of shelf space in the American imagination. I could try to explain why that is so, but there are dozens of other books, films, paintings, Internet message boards, and scholars for that purpose, some of which even agree with each other.

I read books and stories about the battle, and the first historic artifact I ever acquired was an original 1872 crossed-sabers cap insignia, purchased at the New York World's Fair in 1964, identical to what some of the slain troopers might have worn at the battle. My parents dutifully took me to the Little Big Horn battlefield on a family vacation to the Northwest in about 1967, and in later years I attempted to complete a couple of manuscripts that centered on the battle, one of which included an analysis of how close to fact the stanza from Stephen Vincent Benét's poem, about the family whose oldest son died at the Alamo and the youngest with Custer, might be (not close at all). In another I tried to analyze the relative strength of some of the tales of survivors that are part and parcel of the battle's mythology. Also, inevitably, I longed to acquire artifacts from the battle.

Relics of the battle, however, are both plentiful and rare. In the former category are not only those in museums but those still on the battlefield, at least until recently.

In the immediate aftermath of the killing of Custer and five of his twelve companies of cavalry, the Sioux and Cheyenne (along with a handful of Arapahoe) who did the deed removed nearly every useful item from the bodies. Weapons, clothing, hats, saddles, and jewelry were gathered and hauled away. The tops of the soldiers' boots were cut away to be made into moccasin soles, empty brass cartridge cases were picked up for reuse or fashioning into ornaments, and the victors even took the time to cut out the names of the soldiers that were written on their underwear and socks.

The soldiers' practice of writing their names on their clothing was because most looked alike and most went to the same regimental laundry. The Indians' reason for removing the names was probably to add insult to mortal injury by denying the dead recognition by their comrades.

Still, a lot of items were left lying on the field, along with most of the soldiers. Only a handful of the dead were buried. The rest were covered with sagebrush or a sprinkling of dirt until the next year, when the regiment returned to do a better job and to retrieve the bodies of the officers. That the original interments were insufficient was demonstrated by the fact that the reburial and recovery team was only half-confident that it found the body of Custer, who was supposedly the best-buried and most carefully protected of them all. Soldiers' bones have been turning up ever since 1876 and are still not completely accounted for.

Then in 1984 a grass fire swept the battlefield, and the National Park Service decided to use metal detectors and perform an archaeological survey of the site while it was easy to do so. This was wildly successful and led to a great deal of interesting new information about the battle. It also led to a plan to perform additional digs on site and even prompted those conducting the project to issue an invitation to persons interested in assisting.

Besides being a Little Big Horn enthusiast, I was the owner of two or three metal detectors and was somewhat experienced in relic hunting. Naturally I yearned to be a part of the project when I heard about it, but I had a job, as well as two infants at home and a lawyer wife with a full-time career. There was no way I could even apply to assist, let alone go if selected.

Instead, whimsically thinking I could toss a stick on the fire from long range, I wrote a poem about the items I thought might be recovered and mailed it to the address for those interested in applying to assist. I thought perhaps it would come into the hands of a soul mate who would appreciate its sentiment and share it with other like-minded fellows, who might even send me a nod of appreciation. This is it:

LITTLE BIG HORN ARTIFACTS

Come gaze upon these bits of lead
and iron and brass and bone.
Yearn to see what they have seen
and learn what they have known.
They've held their tongues for a hundred years
in the coarse Montana sod,
while men have sought to unlock their tale
known now to none but God.

No plow has touched this Springfield shell
nor concrete hid this broken knife
since they were dropped by frantic men
who fought in vain for life.
No horse this spur has urged to flight;
no belt this buckle held;
each piece has truly held its ground
since their owners each were felled.

For long dark years, their vigil kept,
not touched nor seen by men,
they've awaited those who followed Yates
and rode with Crittenden.
They've awaited those whom last they saw
that 25th of June;
the brothers, Boston, Tom and George
and Margaret's James Calhoun.

Awaited Keogh, with his dancing eyes
and merry Irish laugh;

awaited Cooke with his long sideburns
who served on the colonel's staff;
awaited Harrington, Sturgis, Porter,
three who were never found,
and two hundred more who were fated to die
on Little Big Horn's bloody ground.

But now these relics sing to those
who can hear their silent song,
of moments brief when myths were born,
of mortals, brave but gone.
Come gaze upon these jewels of yore,
once lost and left behind.
Now found, they touch the American heart,
and tease the adventuresome mind.

Several weeks passed, and one day an official-looking letter arrived bearing a return address from the National Park Service headquarters in Montana. I opened it excitedly. Inside a bureaucratic form letter with blanks filled in informed me that my application to participate in the archaeological dig had been denied.

The advent of eBay increased the likelihood that I would be able to obtain artifacts from the battle, even though that particular marketplace is, in the mind of some collectors, synonymous with fakes and counterfeits. As anyone who has used or become addicted to eBay knows, it is like the world's largest flea market. If you can imagine an item's existence, you can probably find some version of it for sale on eBay. Some are treasures and a lot are trash.

A serious collector, of course, must know what to look for and how to spot a fake. Sometimes that is easy; often it is not. There are websites on the Internet that attempt to expose counterfeits and forgeries, but the eBay auctions are usually of limited duration, five to seven days, which doesn't offer much time for significant research about an item that looks and sounds right. The good news about eBay is that it makes thousands of items available for purchase from all over the world in a manner never possible before. The bad news is that, as with life, it comes with no guarantees. A prospective buyer must decide for himself or herself whether to put money at risk to acquire a piece of a dream or simply never to buy anything on eBay, dream or otherwise.

I've been burned way too many times by fakes and counterfeits, mostly in my early days of collecting when I knew what I wanted an item to be but not how to be certain it was as represented. I knew I was gambling by buying anything on eBay, but I'd generally had more good luck than bad and had even found a couple of 7th Cavalry items I was proud to call my own.

One was an officer's crossed-sabers cap insignia with an unusual feature that I'd never seen faked before and that was identical to sets adorning the kepis of well-known officers of the regiment, including Tom Custer, W.W. Cooke, and Algernon Smith. Another was an albumen or cabinet photo of Lt. Edward S. Godfrey.

Godfrey, who lived from 1843 to 1932, commanded Company K at the Little Big Horn, with Benteen's column and Reno's defense, on June 25, 1876. West Point Class of 1867, he was a private in the 21st Ohio Infantry during the Civil War, was with the 7th Cavalry at the Battle of the Washita, kept a diary of the Little Big Horn campaign, was awarded the Medal of Honor for distinguished gallantry at the Battle of Bear Paw Mountain in 1877, and rose to the rank of brigadier general. He served in Cuba during the Spanish American War and wrote four books, including one on the Washita and one on the Little Big Horn. He was even an early collector of Little Big Horn artifacts.

Godfrey played a prominent role at the Battle of the Washita. He led a scouting party downstream from the battle site and discovered that hundreds of more Indians were camped only a few miles away and were gearing up to come after the soldiers. This information convinced Custer to withdraw in an orderly fashion, fighting a rear-guard action as he did so but escaping without experiencing his future fate.

Godfrey was also placed in charge of the fifty-three Cheyenne women and children taken prisoner at the battle, who were mounted on horses culled from the Indian herd before its destruction and placed between the retreating cavalrymen and the trailing hostiles. The day after the battle, en route through the snow to Camp Supply, an older Cheyenne woman who had become the spokesperson for the prisoners asked Godfrey if one of the other women could fall out of the column for awhile. Godfrey was reluctant, but she convinced him that it would only be temporary and that the young woman would return shortly, so he allowed it.

An hour went by and the woman did not return, so Godfrey went to the older squaw [*his* term, now considered a pejorative] and expressed his concern. She laughed at him and, after another hour or so, the missing woman rejoined the column. As Godfrey described it, instead of losing a prisoner he had gained one. The woman had given birth, alone in a snowy pasture, then remounted her horse and ridden to catch up. Next time your wife complains about breaking a fingernail. . . .

In November 2008, my routine eBay search for Little Big Horn artifacts yielded a pleasant surprise. Instead of horseshoe nails found on private land miles from the battlefield, an antiques dealer was offering buttons, bullets, arrowheads, and other items found on or near Last Stand Hill, removed during the 1890s and accompanied by certificates of authenticity and a detailed pedigree.

The items were described as having come from a collection amassed by a man whose grandfather arrived with General Alfred Terry's column two days after the battle and who subsequently lived in South Dakota and recovered numerous artifacts less than twenty years after the battle. They were eventually donated to a museum located in South Dakota, after which the museum encountered financial difficulty, ultimately closing, and sold or deaccessioned the collection, most of which was purchased by the seller's father, who had been a friend of the original collector, the grandson of the veteran.

I bid on a couple of the items and contacted the seller, who was gracious and cooperative and who, in response to my questions, revealed additional, reassuring information about the items he was selling. The collection had been featured, he e-mailed me, in a book written or compiled by his father in 1981. The seller had inherited the collection after his father's death and was selling it off piecemeal, mostly at antique shows and gun shows, where, he wrote, they always received a lot of interest and attention. He only sold them on eBay in advance of the Christmas season and would be putting a few more items up for bid as that holiday approached.

I was tail-wagging excited and decided to purchase all that I could afford, which turned out to be only four items—a musket ball fired or dropped by an Indian, an officer's tunic button, a fork from the Reno portion of the battle, and a copper concha identified as having been attached to a piece of Indian cloth discovered within fifty feet of the spot where Custer had been found.

I also acquired, from different sellers, two 1876 newspapers featuring a firsthand report, as well as a Thomas Nast cartoon about the massacre, and a war club and an arrow manufactured in modern times by Lakota artisans, the latter having been made for the movie *Dances with Wolves*. Including a Springfield cartridge case and fired bullet found not far from the battlefield, along with three crossed-saber cap insignias of different makes, I had enough to mount a pretty impressive shadow-box display, which I set about to do.

I also attempted to have a friendly e-mail conversation with the seller in the hope that he might reward my interest with an offer of one or more items not yet placed on eBay. Instead, after two or three exchanges of messages, he became terse and his replies sporadic. The change was noteworthy, so I retraced my messages to see if I might have said something objectionable. In my message following his last friendly one, I had concluded by saying that if he wanted to "verify my bona fides" he could "Google" me. As a lawyer and an author, my name managed to wind up on the Internet in several places, and I had thought that if the seller realized I was potentially solvent and serious about both history and the law, he might decide I was a customer worthy of his commerce. Instead, the new tone of his communication caused me to worry about *his* bona fides.

He had written that he owned two copies of his father's book, although they were packed away and not handy, and that the last time he had seen one sell, at a gun show, it had fetched $500. He had told me that the items he was selling were included in the book, so I naturally wanted to get a copy or at least a photocopy of the relevant pages to lend credence to the provenance of my new acquisitions. I'd inquired about the possibility of acquiring photocopies and suggested that including them with the items he was selling would enhance their marketability, but he did not reply.

So I decided to find it elsewhere and called the Austin Public Library to make certain it was listed in Books in Print and then to order a copy on interlibrary loan.

You know where this is headed. The book was not in BIP, nor did any library list it. Two different book-finder firms found no trace, either as a mainstream publication or as a self-published work. The publisher in New York had no record of it.

I began tracing the seller's other leads. Turns out the original owner's "veteran" grandfather, or the person whom the seller suggested was that man, had arrived at the battlefield on June 28, 1876, and was an officer who was one of the first to see Custer's dead. He was killed the following year, however, in 1877, leaving behind a daughter and a pregnant widow who subsequently gave birth to another daughter. It wasn't very likely he would have had a grandson with the same last name.

Branching out, I contacted local officials in South Dakota, searching for the museum to which the items had supposedly been donated and from which they were later deaccessioned. A lot of phone calls to state and local officials, plus inquiries to a Little Big Horn–related message board finally revealed that a state bank in a South Dakota town with a name similar to that of the museum had once had a collection of Native American artifacts on display. When I tracked down the owner of the collection, who was the son of the man who put it together, he had no record or recollection of anything that came close to matching the eBay seller's claims and descriptions.

I e-mailed the author of a book on Custer artifacts, told him the story, and asked his opinion. He was gracious but advised that none of the claims matched information with which he was familiar. His advice was to "be cautious and to buy things because they are what they are supposed to be and not what you would like them to be." Well, duh!

I'd been screwed.

The matter mushroomed further thereafter. I was contacted by other people who either had unhappy dealings with the same seller or who had observed his advertisements and suspected fraud. One had spent several thousand dollars, had gotten to know the man, then became suspicious about stories the seller told him about formerly being a law enforcement officer, checked into the story, and found no support for it.

E-mail exchanges with the seller were initially fruitless but somewhat entertaining. The man was not a good speller, and at one point in our discussions I asked, "Why not provide me with something more than your word? Photocopy of the book? Names of the museums? My preference is to learn the relics are genuine, but all I can find is your claim." He responded "I am not going to drop names and get my butt sued because someone like you harrases them, they dont give out my name ?? I am not going to give personal info out on my father. He was a very important man and my family life is PRIVATE. I sold at [a] gun show this last weekend and sold 7 of my items there and ALL were 100% happy and satisfied after meeting me and knowing my reputation and edgucation."

One should be careful dealing with a man who is well edgucated.

Belatedly I realized that PayPal, through which I had purchased the items, had a policy of refunding money when claims of fraud could be proven, and I filed a claim that they investigated and approved but only for the fourth of the four items which had been purchased less than sixty days before the claim was filed. Nevertheless, before PayPal made its decision and after other dissatisfied buyers joined the chorus of complaints to the seller, the seller surrendered and sent a rather pathetic message:

> Hello Mr. Akers, I get a pension at the end of each month, which this
> month will be Feb 25. I will send you a full refund for your items,
> excluding the pending decision on the knife item of $178.34 that is
> in Paypal. Paypal has till Feb 25 to make a decision whether you get
> the refund or not. If you are the "winner" of their decision, you will
> get paid for your 4th item through Paypal, if they rule in my favor, I
> will send you the $178.34 with the other 3 item payment. I will send
> you the balance via USPS postal money order, registered mail with
> signature required. I will email you when the letter is in the mail. Total
> including your shipping is $888.
>
> If you agree to letting me pay you on Feb 25 with my pension
> money, I will pay in full.

I agreed, of course, and he didn't pay, of course. Ultimately another buyer and I were able to get refunds through the credit/debit card companies through which we had paid PayPal, but the buyer who had lost the most money and who had checked into the seller's law enforcement background got nothing. Consumer fraud complaints to the state attorney general's office yielded an investigation but no prosecution. As far as I know the man is still selling at shows and on eBay items which are accompanied by certificates of authenticity and claims of great historical significance, although he has closed out the eBay account he used previously and the significant historic artifacts he is now selling are from World War II instead of the Little Big Horn. I periodically receive an e-mail from someone else who has fallen victim to him or who knows someone who has and found me on the Little Big Horn website where I made inquiries and shared my story. One lady contacted me and said she was desperate to help a friend who, she related, had gone in debt $85,000 buying items from the man. I told them what I knew, empathized, agreed that something needs to be done, and sent follow-up messages to the state attorney general's office, which is supposedly keeping a file open on the man.

The cloudy experience had a bit of a silver lining, in that I came in contact during my "investigation" with others who were interested in artifacts from the Little Big Horn, two of whom were able and willing to provide me with a few battle relics with reliable pedigrees, so that the shadow-box display I'd planned ultimately went up on a wall. Considering the track record I described above, I don't know why anyone would believe me when I say that the pedigrees of those latter relics are reliable, but hey, I am only trying to sell this story, not the relics, and we all know the story is trash.

10

Trashing Marble

I hate the man who builds his name on
the ruins of another's fame.
JOHN GAY, 1688–1733

AMERICANS TODAY ARE ACCUSTOMED TO HEARING AND READING STORIES
that criticize, defame, scandalize, and ridicule our leaders, entertainers,
sports heroes, and virtually any noteworthy human who ambles into the
gun sights of a story-hungry tabloid or reporter. Whether a person is president or pope, he or she is not immune to juicy gossip or downright lies about
things he or she did, said, thought, or might have done, said, or thought.

That was not so much the tradition in earlier times. Of course there
were thousands of juicy scandals revealed, accusations made, and duels
fought over private matters made public about famous people, but for the
most part folks were better behaved when it came to destroying each others'
reputations just for the fun of it than they are in the twenty-first century.

Nearly every historical character of note has had his or her detractors
and wannabe Woodwards and Bernsteins. Few of the world's greatest have
escaped some sort of shocking analysis, revelation, or accusation, true or

speculative, whether it be that Abraham Lincoln was homosexual, Thomas Jefferson had a black mistress, or that Mother Teresa had sacrilegious thoughts.

One of the few who has escaped almost all significant criticism and scandal, however, is Robert E. Lee. To the contrary, Lee has always been and still is the "marble man," possessing such noble qualities, military genius, devotion to duty and God, and being so "magnificent in defeat" that Americans have always and will probably always continue to place him on a pedestal. He is revered above hundreds of other great men and women, as well he should be.

Certainly books and periodical articles have taken Lee to task for military mistakes, defense of slavery, and that pesky chain of events associated with an army he commanded that nearly destroyed the United States, but these are usually presented as scholarly, historical analyses. What is surprising is that no one has decided to tear into his image and try, with full-blown *National Enquirer* persistence and absence of skill, to simply lay the man low.

Take for example, the fact that he had seven children, all of whom lived to adulthood but only two of whom ever married. One of his sons and all of his daughters, with one exception, lived full, longish lives without ever taking a spouse. The exception was Annie, who died in 1862 at age twenty-three, certainly past marrying age for the time but young enough to be given a pass on whatever speculations about homosexuality or parental dysfunction might be conjured up.

Another daughter, Agnes, died in 1873 at age thirty-two, but by then she would have been a full-blown candidate for spinsterhood by the standards of the day. Mary lived to be eighty-three, Milly, fifty-nine, and Custis, eighty-one, all without mates or at least without those of traditional gender relationship that was within public knowledge. Only sons Rooney and Robert, Jr., married, two times apiece, and had children.

Why hasn't some enterprising journalist, images of a Pulitzer dancing in his or her head, set out to prove either that Robert E. Lee caused most of his children to grow up gay or that his Christ-like personality or some secret pedophilia made them incapable of finding a suitable mate?

And if no one is inclined in that direction, why has no one decided to accuse General Lee of being an outright traitor?

Oh sure, there were several hundreds of thousands of accusations of that sort made in the year 1861 and shortly thereafter, but the question here is, why has no one suggested that Lee was a traitor to the Confederacy? Why has no jackass alleged that he either intentionally, secretly, or psycho-somatically sold his young nation down the river?

Lack of historical support for the suggestion may be one answer or the prospect of a howling lynch mob of pitchfork-waving southerners could be another, but when have such factors stopped the truly irresponsible?

If one were inclined to explore such a hypothesis, one would inevitably begin with the fact that Lee had to agonize, sweat blood, and tear out pieces of his soul in order to decide to follow his native Virginia out of his beloved Union. That surely would have left a mark.

Next one might point to how wildly reckless Lee was with command of the army whose avowed purpose was to protect and bring victory to his government. On numerous occasions, particularly Malvern Hill, Second Manassas, Sharpsburg, and Chancellorsville, he defied all military logic and reason in order to fight battles in a manner that seemed destined to fail. He ordered headlong frontal assaults against massed artillery, divided his forces in the face of superior numbers, directed insanely risky flank marches and attacks, stood his ground on unfamiliar soil against an army three times the size of his, and made attacks against superior numbers that no modern computer video game would allow to succeed. Yet succeed he did.

Then there is Gettysburg. First he ignored the advice of his most trusted lieutenant, James Longstreet, who suggested a course of action—get between the Union army and Washington, D.C., dig in on high ground, and force them to attack—that seems unimpeachable today. Then he launched a massive, suicidal frontal assault against an entrenched enemy on high ground, Fredericksburg-like, and provided his doomed division commanders with no supporting troops to capitalize on success if it had inexplicably occurred, which it nearly did. Doesn't seem prudent.

On a personal level, Lee attempted or contemplated military suicide on at least three occasions, twice at the Battle of the Wilderness and once at Saylors Creek, when he attempted to lead an attack or seized a Confederate flag and made a tempting target of himself. Only the intervention of protective officers and enlisted men prevented him from becoming a Yankee infantryman's sweet dream of a target. At the end of the siege of Petersburg, he remarked that it would be so easy to end it all, just by riding along the lines and allowing himself to be shot. Was he feeling guilty about something?

Certainly he jumped at the chance to blame himself, riding among his defeated men after Pickett's Charge and again after Appomattox, saying things like "It is all my fault." He also took lousy care of himself, not eating as well as he could have, sleeping on a narrow cot in a drafty tent, even though he knew there was something wrong with his health, heart trouble maybe, and that his nation needed him to be in top physical condition. Stonewall Jackson was a fanatic about his health but not Lee. Lee sometimes acted like he wanted to die.

At the end of the war, given the opportunity to do as his president expected and allow his army to break up, head for the hills or toward other southern armies still in the field, fighting as bushwhackers and guerrillas, prolonging the war and the quest for victory as long as possible, he refused. It seems noble now, martyr-like, but was it something else?

Then there is the physical evidence.

Despite being a full general, one of only eight in the Confederate armies, Lee refused to wear the insignia of that rank. Instead he chose to wear three stars, which denoted the rank of colonel, the highest rank he ever held in the United States Army. Other general officers did not do that. In fact, had a subordinate refused to wear his correct rank, Lee probably would have chastised him and explained the military importance of exhibiting correct insignia so that other officers and soldiers would recognize the officer in order to obey orders and carry out their duties. He might have pointed out that wearing insignia of rank beneath that actually held yet expecting everyone to recognize an officer's true rank merely by recognizing his appearance was unacceptably egotistical and vain. These were not traits Lee is remembered for, yet for some reason Lee felt as though he was above that simple military convention or duty. What was that all about?

Another telling incident occurred after the war. Living in Lexington, Virginia, serving as president of Washington College, he frequently came in contact with the cadets at the neighboring Virginia Military Institute. Yet when they marched nearby, Lee would consistently and intentionally walk out of step with the marching cadence of the passing drums and soldiers. He admitted doing so, even telling a friend of it and remarking that he considered joining the military to be one of the greatest mistakes of his life.

What the. . . . ?

But the purpose of this speculative little piece of yellow journalism is not to accuse Lee of being a failure or traitor, either as a military leader or as family man, but to reveal something easier to prove and only slightly less shocking: Robert E. Lee was bald.

Before the cawing cacophony of cries and denials gains volume, it should be pointed out that this is not necessarily a bad thing. It is often said that minority children and others in disadvantaged situations desperately need role models, and it is true. Yet rarely does anyone realize that bald men need them too, just as much and maybe more so. Surely bald men are some of the most disadvantaged, confidence-shaken, and abused of citizens. How sweet it would be, how backbone-restoring, if baldies could but point to General Robert E. Lee and say, "See, bald as an egg, just like me." How many generations might have prospered, how many diseases might have been cured, how many nations might have avoided war and pestilence? How different the world might be.

As proof, consider the following.

The earliest known photograph of Lee was taken in 1845 when Lee was thirty-eight. He poses, with mutton chops but neither moustache nor beard, with his young son Rooney. His hair is dark, parted low on one side of his head and combed straight and horizontally to the other side in classic comb-over style. Now examine each of the thirty-five other known photos of the man, including the most recently discovered, which was published in the 2008 edition of the *Confederate Calendar,* produced in Austin, Texas, by Lawrence T. Jones III, since 1975.

Many of the photos are on the Internet or in various biographies of him or other Civil War books. If one has access to Roy Meredith's 1981 book, *The Face of Robert E. Lee in Life and in Legend,* peruse the photos in chronological order, along with various portraits, sculptures and variations of the known photos. Rarely will one find an image that doesn't suggest comb-over. Some, such as an 1864 photo by J. Vannerson depicting Lee in profile, one taken by Mathew Brady shortly after Appomattox, and the three taken by Mathew Brady in May 1869, practically *scream* comb-over. It is a good comb-over, as many are, but a comb-over just the same.

More telling is Lee's death mask. It may be found on the Internet or on page 102 of Meredith's book, and copies may even be for sale somewhere

Photograph of Robert E. Lee taken by Mathew Brady in Richmond a few days after Appomattox. The image is consistent with an Appomattox witness's statement that Lee was "quite bald" and was wearing "one of the side locks of his hair thrown across the upper portion of his forehead. . . ." Reprinted by permission of Virginia Military Institute Archives.

The death mask of Robert E. Lee. Although the hair of his beard, moustache, and "side locks" is visible, the top of his head appears to be bare. Reprinted by permission of the Museum of the Confederacy, Richmond, Virginia.

on eBay. It depicts a man with a moustache and beard and with what is obviously hair around his ears, but who is bowling-ball bald on top. Swear.

As the pièce de la résistance, consider the following quote from an unidentified observer at the McLean House at Appomattox, reported in the January 2006 *Civil War Times* magazine on page 76:

> Lee arrived first, looking to one observer "quite bald" and wearing "one of the side locks of his hair thrown across the upper portion of his forehead, which is as white and as fair as a woman's."

Lee combed over like a used-car salesman. The aging-badly, can't-afford-a-transplant, think-they're-fooling-everybody, unrehabilitated Rudy Giulianis of the world have a soul mate in Robert E. Lee.

Oh, the humanity.

Which also means that when that valiant courier riding hard with dispatches from General Stuart, containing oh-so-important information about the location of the enemy, knocked on his tent pole and was greeted by a night-shirted Lee fumbling with his spectacles, the young trooper would have also seen General Lee with his side flap hanging straight down.

And General Lee in the heat of battle, mounted on Traveler, hat in hand, exhorting the gallant men of the Army of Northern Virginia forward, ever forward, follow your general, with them shouting, "Lee to the rear; Lee to the rear," that side flap was probably standing straight out in the wind like a one-winged albatross.

The boys may not have been worried so much that General Lee would be shot but that Grant's men to see that shiny dome and snow-white head and would learn the terrible truth.[17]

How the dreams of youth do crumble with age. If it were not ignominious enough to have only folks like Richard Ewell and Ambrose Burnside as Civil War role models, baldies now must learn that we could have had the man himself . . . but no. The bald are and will remain cursed.

11

Artifacts and Attitudes

Thus times do shift, each thing his turn does hold; new things
succeed, and former things grow old.
ROBERT HERRICK, 1591–1674

IN CASE THE CHAPTER ABOUT CUSTER AND COMANCHE WAS INSUFFICIENT
to suggest to readers that the collecting of artifacts is risky or that my expertise in recognizing genuine items is spotty at best, let me attempt to solidify
both suggestions further.

The American Civil War is considered by many people to be our nation's most intriguing time period. There are numerous reasons for this, but
as with the country's fascination with Custer and the Little Big Horn, it is
best left to other books and other authors for explanations.

Baby Boomers had the centennial of the war, 1961–1965, to draw their
attention. Coming at an exciting time—the election of John Kennedy and a
seemingly brilliant American future, and only slightly on the heels of *Gone
with the Wind* fantasy, the old tales of Lincoln, Lee, Gettysburg, the Lost
Cause, and saving the Union seemed eternally fresh and were heady stuff
for lots of folks. To be sure, many in the South embraced it and some of its

worn-out racial notions in reaction to the Civil Rights movement, but there weren't any rules that said you had to be intelligent or enlightened to be attracted to it. Authors like Bruce Catton and the *Life* magazine multi-week series of articles on the war fanned other flames. It is a period of American history that will always be popular, and it was particularly so for folks who grew up in the 1950s and 1960s.

Personally, the war first entered my realm of existence two miles out of Higgins, Texas, population 700, because my then best friend, Jerry Steinle, and I liked to pretend to be soldiers and play with toy guns, circa 1957–1962, but we both wanted simultaneously to be enemies of each other as well as be Americans. We were not particularly xenophobic, but we each wanted to stalk and make war on the other with cowboy-type six-guns as military men rather than as outlaws or Indians. The Civil War, once we learned what it was, seemed custom-made for our purposes.

In 1958, one of my two older sisters, Pam, aged sixteen, won a statewide speech contest sponsored by the Order of Odd Fellows. She and the teen-aged winners from other states were rewarded with a bus tour of speech-making across the eastern United States, including stops at Washington, D.C., New York City, and Gettysburg. She brought me back a bag of book-lets, pamphlets, and postcards from the latter site and set the hook more firmly. The centennial followed, and I was done for.

By the time I was in high school, I had become so devoted to the Civil War that the local American history teachers utilized my passion for short respites from work. When I was a sophomore, I was given a class period to lecture my classmates on the Civil War. As a junior it was expanded to three classes over two days. By the time I was a senior the other teachers had caught on, and I was given a full week in the school auditorium to inflict my knowledge of the subject, and obvious nerd status, on the combined junior- and senior-high history classes.

Something I consider ironic, rather disturbing, and yet notable, is that since I was first old enough to understand what the Civil War was, I have been fiercely pro-southern in my attitudes and interests whereas now, in my golden years, I am convinced that the southern cause was an abomination.

For many years I tried to ignore the pesky issue of slavery in connection with what the Confederate States of America tried to do. Later I tried to rationalize and theorize that most of the horrific racial trouble and hate the United States has experienced arose out of post–Civil War reaction as the South tried to defeat reconstruction. Nobody in their right mind would attempt to justify or defend either slavery or racism, and what intrigued me about the southern cause were its leaders, its gallantry, and the grit of its fighting men, plus a healthy dose of *Gone with the Wind* fantasy about life in the Old South.

About 1986, in fact, I attempted to express my attitude in a poem or set of song lyrics called "The Southern Birthright," which went like this:

There's a birthright that each southern boy inherits when he's born,
and he carries it forever, 'til the day his mourners mourn.
It's not founded in old politics of race or slavery,
and those who see no more than that are blind to history.

Chorus:
For our hearts are still with Jackson
and our faith's in General Lee,
and we still can taste the sweetness
of that one last victory.
Though we'll never ride with Forrest
and we'll never march with Bragg,
we will love our southern heroes
and the old Confederate flag.

It's the way of life that ended and the way it died so hard.
It's the honor and the chivalry folks today most disregard.
It's the ride around McClellan and New Market's young cadets.
It's Sam Watkins tellin' stories, and Sam Davis's regrets.

Chorus: And our hearts are still with Longstreet
and our faith's in General Lee.
We still can taste the sweetness
of that one last victory.
And though we'll never ride with Stuart
nor march with Braxton Bragg,
We will love our southern heroes
and the old Confederate flag.

It's the thought of Pickett charging and never being stopped.
It's the dream of Stonewall Jackson never being shot.
Oh, we wouldn't change America—she is as she should be—
but we still think we're good enough for one more victory.

Chorus:
For our hearts are still with A.P. Hill
and our faith's in Bobby Lee.
In our dreams we still see them march
and pass by silently.
We'll never ride with Hampton,
nor be caught with Granny Bragg
but we'll love our southern birthright,
and the old Confederate flag.

A talented musician named Bobby Horton liked the lyrics and put them to music, first providing the song as background for a local documentary video, *Above the Wind*, about the burial of a Confederate soldier killed at the battle of Kennesaw Mountain, Georgia, whose skeleton was discovered by a relic hunter in 1988 and was interred with full Confederate honors at the Confederate Cemetery in Marietta, Georgia, on April 29, 1989. Horton then included it on the sixth volume of his CDs titled *Homespun Songs of the C.S.A.*, released in 2001. The song has even been incorporated into two different YouTube videos.[14]

The reason I find the foregoing disturbing rather than gratifying is because this nation's experience from 2000 to 2009, during which it launched a misguided war in Iraq, suffered great loss of image and reputation around the world, and learned of political and business scandals of gargantuan proportions, while resulting in a laudable reversal and election of a charismatic leader, has also divided and polarized people, seemingly as much or more than that which occurred in connection with Vietnam, Watergate, or the impeachment of President Bill Clinton. The division of attitudes seems sharper than at any time since the Civil War, and it simply must pass and settle down. Of course political attitudes differ, and of course the party that supported those failed policies will deny responsibility, but one cannot wonder if we are not witnessing a bit of what the nation witnessed in 1860.

Abraham Lincoln is remembered as the greatest U.S. president who ever lived, and his leadership in bringing an end to slavery and preserving the Union was, in my opinion, the pivotal, catalytic event that decided that the United States would become the most powerful country in the world instead of a handful of bickering neighbor nations. Had the Confederacy been successful, it is unlikely that it would have been the last group of states to pack up its toys and go home. It is pretty unlikely, in fact, that the eleven states that made up the CSA could have hung together for more than a few years before Texas, Virginia, Louisiana, or Florida decided it needed to strike out on its, or their, own.

Accordingly, while I still feel pride in my southern heritage and am drawn to relics of the Confederacy, I know that had I lived in 1860 my sympathies would have been with the Union. Furthermore, despite having written and still being a believer in the sentiments expressed in "The Southern Birthright," I'm afraid that many of its admirers miss the point. It is the lines "[i]t's not founded in old politics of race or slavery" and "we wouldn't change America—she is as she should be" that convey the message of the lyrics, and anyone who admires both it and the message delivered by hate radio programs is missing that message. The idea is we can and must accept and find reason to be proud of our respective heritages but not by clinging to and trying to revive failed or repugnant policies and not by denying the truth of our past.

Stepping down from that soapbox, let me observe that there are several different avenues a person can take who feels a need to devote a significant portion of his life to a historic period, such as the Civil War. Reading and research are obvious, as is movie-going, but there is also re-enacting, relic hunting, and collecting, Civil War music, writing, and, apparently, even Civil War poetry. I tried them all at one time or another and all still have their charms, but there is something about acquiring an artifact of the period that most tugs at my heartstrings and my bank account.

I did not start collecting seriously until about 1974, when I discovered relic boards put together by a retired army colonel from Dallas named Ed Moore. Colonel Moore, who was a West Point grad, father of a general, and a dead-ringer for Colonel Harland Sanders of KFC fame, would purchase Civil War finds in bulk from Virginia relic hunters and then arrange and mount them on antiqued boards with identifications of each item and its place of recovery on a paper lacquered to the back. I bought several.

Actual relic hunting followed, but purchasing items from other collectors became a mainstay preoccupation. Eventually, several hundred items passed through my hands. A couple of bouts of hard economic times of a personal nature depleted the collection, but it always grew back when times became prosperous again. I have certainly not learned all I need to know about the science of collecting authentic artifacts, but I have picked up an understanding of the emotions of collecting them. One tenet is that owning a nice artifact is never as exciting as finding one for sale that you can't afford. Another is that the joy of owning a really good artifact never counterbalances the despair of learning it is a fake. Third is that neither owning a good item nor learning that one you were proud of is counterfeit is as emotionally intense as recalling a good one you once owned that you later sold for peanuts.

What I own today is far from being a world-class display, but some of the pieces have stories to tell and, as with the letters, those stories represent the real joy of collecting.

There is, for example, a small game-set box that was manufactured to look like two books and is labeled on its spine as being the *History of America, Volume 1* and *Volume 2*. The checkered leather binding, when the box is opened on its hinges on the spine, serves as a checkerboard. On the other side, inside the little box, is a backgammon game and red-and-white pieces that serve as both checkers and backgammon pieces. The previous owner also wrote a letter on most of the pieces that correspond with chess pieces, K for king, P for pawn, etc., and also penciled in numbers in corners of the checkerboard squares. One can theorize that this was for the purpose of allowing players to jot down the location of their chess pieces when something interrupted a game.

The man who was probably the original owner also stenciled his name inside the box: "Wm Downey, 4 Reg., MS. Cav." Downey, a little research revealed, was a private in Company B of the 4th Massachusetts Cavalry. He was from Falls River, Massachusetts, which later produced a famous daughter named Lizzie Borden. He was thirty when he enlisted on September 24, 1863, was wounded and taken prisoner on August 17, 1864, was paroled, and mustered out on June 17, 1865.

Where Downey's and the game box's story gets good is the discovery that he was a recipient of the Medal of Honor. He "[v]olunteered as a member of a boat crew which went to the rescue of a large number of Union soldiers on board the stranded steamer *Boston,* and with great gallantry assisted in conveying them to shore, being exposed during the entire time to a heavy fire from a Confederate battery."[19]

The *Boston* was a steam-powered side-wheeler built by Bell and Brown of New York in 1850. Before the war she plied the Atlantic from her namesake city to Portland, Maine, and later carried passengers and freight between New York City and Philadelphia. When the war began, the ship was converted to a troop transport and served in various campaigns, first taking troops from New York to Annapolis, then operating off of South Carolina, Georgia, and Florida.

On May 24, 1864, the *Boston* was on the Ashepoo River in South Carolina as part of a joint Army-Navy operation under the command of General John Porter Hatch. The operation's goal was to burn a railroad bridge that spanned the river. The *Boston* was captained by F.M. Fairchild and had on board 300 members of the 34th U.S. Colored Troops, commanded by Colonel James Montgomery, and about 100 members of the 4th Massachusetts, as well as ninety-one horses.

She was delayed in embarking from Mosquito Inlet, where the troops loaded, because she was a deep-draft vessel, and the troops had to be carried to her from shore in smaller boats. When she was ordered to steam away that evening, about a third of the 34th Regiment was left behind, and only one small rowboat was taken along.

The night was dark and foggy, and the ship made only about five miles before it hit an oyster bed and became firmly stranded. A small Union gunboat came along and advised Colonel Montgomery to send over twenty-five men to serve as sharpshooters to prevent the Confederates from planting a battery and shelling the ship. These twenty-five men were selected from the 4th Massachusetts and were sent away toward the gunboat, along with four lone cavalrymen from another regiment of Regulars, all armed with Spencer repeating rifles. They were under the command of Lt. George W. Brush of the 34th and were put in the one small boat that had been brought along from Mosquito Inlet.

Before the men in the rowboat reached the gunboat, however, a Confederate battery opened fire on the *Boston*. Then when the rowboat reached the gunboat, its captain decided it would be improper for him to "take undue risks" by hanging around. Lieutenant Brush stood up in the small boat, and as soon as the rest of his men were on the gunboat, he called for volunteers to join him in rescuing the 400 men stranded on the doomed *Boston*. Four men volunteered, one of whom was Private William Downey of Falls River.

Turmoil had set in on board the *Boston*. Rebel shells were finding their mark, soldiers were beginning to jump overboard to swim for it, and the horses had begun to panic. As the rowboat pulled alongside, Colonel Montgomery shouted, "Lieutenant, everything now depends on you. Yours is the only boat we have!"

Nearly thirty soldiers crowded onto the little boat but did not swamp it, and the four volunteers began the arduous task of ferrying them to shore, then turning around and doing it again. As Brush wrote later, "[t]he enemy continued their firing, with our boat as their chief target. Now and then a shot would kill a man and several times we came near foundering; but at last we got them all safely ashore."[20]

The horses could not be saved and to keep the ship and its stores from falling into enemy hands, the boat crew set the *Boston* afire when the last of the soldiers was off. She burned to the water's edge. Brush and the four volunteers later became "Medal of Honor Men" for their work that day.

On June 2, 1979, two divers named Howard Tower and Larry Tipping located the *Boston's* remains. They obtained a salvage license and under the supervision of the South Carolina State Underwater Archaeologist, they excavated the ship and recovered various artifacts, including quite a few horse bones and hooves. Because the wreck was covered with silt, several soft items that would have rotted away on land were found intact.

In one of those odd little quirks that sometimes happens, a few years after I acquired Private Downey's game box, I purchased some items from the ship—a button, a small piece of rope, a small piece of cloth, a grommet, and a brass "34" that was once affixed to the cabin of that number—but without making a mental connection between the two events or the artifacts. A couple of years later, I happened to reread the certificate of authenticity that came with the *Boston* items and something clicked. I rushed to my notes on William Downey and realized that the handful of items that had once shared an exciting spring day in South Carolina had been reunited in Texas after nearly 125 years.

Downey returned to Falls River and remained in the area until his death in 1909. He would have been around to hear the buzz of gossip about that gruesome murder down at 92 Second Street on August 4, 1892, and to speculate about whether the victims' daughter/stepdaughter was really the murderer. He is buried in Section 10, Lot 147 of Saint Mary's Cemetery in New Bedford.

Not all artifacts yield such a complete story. Like most collectors, I was initially attracted to what I considered to be more showy items and laid out some serious cash for a genuine Confederate shell jacket and kepi sold at a Houston gun show. The jacket certainly seemed to tell a story, and I was able to piece together something I considered to be quite fascinating to tell any visitor who made the mistake of asking about it. Ultimately, however, my research began to suggest authenticity problems, so I contacted the Museum of the Confederacy and asked if I could submit it for examination, after which I was told it was probably a costume piece from the turn of the century. I wound up selling it as such at another gun show, accurately identified, for about a tenth of what I paid for it.

However, even being cheated or being a sucker can have lead to interesting results. The discovery that the shell jacket was not genuine caused me to think the Confederate kepi I had purchased at the same time was suspect as well, so, for practical rather than romantic purposes, I took it with me on my honeymoon to Virginia and wound up trading it to a dealer in Harper's Ferry in return for an ambrotype of a genuine, by-golly Confederate soldier. I knew it was good because the soldier in the photo was wearing a distinctive cap I'd seen on several published photos of Rebels.

Subsequent research on that item, however, revealed that the genuine Confederate just happened to be a member of a Yankee New Hampshire regiment that wore gray uniforms at the beginning of the war. The saving grace was that the peculiar headgear the soldier was wearing led to an article titled "That Crazy Cap" (the editor's choice of title, not mine) published in the January–February 1984 issue of *Military Images* magazine. That article, in turn, prompted another collector to submit and have published an article in the May–June 1984 issue of the same magazine, titled

"Whipple's Patent Military Cap," which is what the crazy cap was. In 2009 I was contacted by an author who was preparing to publish a two-volume set of books on uniforms of the Civil War. He wanted to publish the photo I acquired on my honeymoon, as well as another in my possession. Interestingly, he lives in England.

The connect-the-dots series of events associated with the counterfeit shell jacket led to another, less-gratifying bunny trail. Shortly after I acquired it and while I still believed it to be genuine, I was contacted by another Civil War enthusiast I'd met in Houston who asked if he could bring over a friend who was an expert on Confederate uniforms to examine it. They listened to my proud little tale of what certain parts of it told me, made some complimentary remarks that seemed forced to me, and left, after which I'm sure they guffawed with glee over my naïveté and lack of knowledge. This same enthusiast also served in the Texas re-enactor unit, participated in the political scheming described in a preceding chapter, and then became a lawyer. When last I heard of him, he was serving as legal counsel and spokesman for the Aryan Nation, as hardcore a group of racist idiots as ever sullied the image of America or the South. Any embarrassment he contributed to my belief in the fake jacket is more than offset by the universal humiliation he deserves for associating with that group.[21]

Another heartbreaker of a counterfeit I purchased early on in my collecting career was a rectangular CSA belt plate. Confederate items are more rare and more valuable than their Federal counterparts, despite their association with folks whose politics are despicable. So when I ran across the belt plate, in the hands of a relic dealer from Virginia, for sale at a Houston gun show, I scraped together my life savings and frolicked home with it. It took me a few years to learn it was a fake.

I also learned that the Virginia relic dealer I'd purchased it from had established a reputation for chicanery and fraud that was so well known among collectors in the eastern United States that he may have been forced to come to Texas just to find new fools to fleece, at which he was quite successful where I was concerned.

That was not to say that he did not find, acquire, and keep some genuine, enviable items of his own, however, and in the 1990s he opened a museum and relic shop near the site of a well-known Virginia battlefield.

On a vacation in Virginia, my family decided to visit his museum and viewed some fine items, including a letter from my own first cousin four times removed, Reuben Cornelius Akers, who was a VMI cadet wounded at the Battle of New Market. I sighed and, to commemorate my fleecing of some fifteen years previously, wrote a note in the museum's visitors' log that went something like this: "John. Wonderful relics, but I sure wish you hadn't sold me that fake Confederate belt plate in Houston back in 1974."

My son, learning in the car what I had done, had to see for himself and reentered the museum to look at the visitor's log. However, the museum's proprietor had gotten there first. My entry had been partially redacted and revised so that it read something like "John, Wonderful relics, but I sure wish you had sold me more like that Confederate belt plate in Houston back in 1974."

History can be pliable in some people's hands, even when it is newly hatched.

A few of the items in my collection, although a lot fewer than I would like, did not cost me anything, at least directly, because I recovered them myself, using a metal detector. I obtained my first detector while still in high school and found a few items between then and law school. During my first year at the University of Houston, in 1974, I became interested in locating and hunting the site of Camp Groce, a Confederate prison camp, for Yankees that is, located near Hempstead, Texas, about thirty miles from Houston. My ad in a newspaper seeking information was answered by a long-time relic hunter who just happened to be looking not only for Camp Groce but a new relic-hunting buddy. We teamed up and with him I was able to experience some real relic hunting, or as real as it was possible to experience in the 1970s and early 1980s.

There are, I'm convinced, still plenty of artifacts in the ground to be recovered, but it is necessary to find the right place, get permission, not run afoul of an outraged archaeologist-type who considers metal detecting to be synonymous with raping and pillaging, and then get lucky. As of the late 1970s, most of the places where relics were known to lurk were already hunted out or prohibited metal detectors. My new buddy, Patrick, had helped hunt a lot of them out, having been in the hobby for nearly twenty years, but he still knew a few sites to show me in Texas, Louisiana, Arkansas, and Mississippi, and I was an apt and appreciative student.

During the next eight or ten years, before Patrick and I moved away from each other and lost contact, he took me on numerous adventures and, although I never recovered anything rare and precious, he had done so, and we found enough together to make the memories sweet. Once, at a War of 1812 site in Mississippi, one of the very first signals I dug turned out to be a Spanish one-real silver coin dated 1776. It was not and is not particularly valuable but sitting there in the woods looking at it, knowing it had not been seen by another human for about 160 years, was a thrill.

On another occasion we stumbled onto a small area on a Civil War battlefield that had not been hunted out and recovered five live artillery projectiles, duds that had not exploded when they were fired into the Confederate lines in 1863. Patrick knew a man who was willing to defuse them in return for one of them, as payment for risking his life.

Another time Patrick went on a hunt at the same battlefield when I was unable to go and returned to report that he got a signal that turned out to be the tin inserts to a cartridge box, still filled with minie balls. Then he found a Federal U.S. belt plate, a handful of brass buttons, some hobnails, a keeper buckle from a kepi strap, and it occurred to him that the small chalky, white rocks he was also uncovering were not rocks at all but human bone fragments.

Another item in my collection that I did not find and about which the jury is still out is a cannonball from the Battle of San Jacinto.

There were only three cannon on the field of that famous battle fought on April 21, 1836, that won independence for Texas. Two, called the Twin Sisters, were on the Texian side. They were six-pounders, a gift from supporters of Texas independence in Ohio. The third, and only artillery piece on site in Santa Anna's army, was a brass gun, believed to be a twelve-pounder that was given the name, the Golden Standard.

The Mexican army in Texas certainly had other artillery pieces and had used them effectively in the siege of the Alamo, but Santa Anna had divided his forces in his headlong pursuit of the retreating Texians and had only the one cannon with the force under his personal command that, he believed would bring Houston's 800 men to ground near the San Jacinto River on April 20.

The Golden Standard was only fired three times, mostly grapeshot, during the actual battle and was being prepared for a fourth shot when a round from one of the Twin Sisters hit its water bucket, stunned its gunners, and allowed the attacking Texians to capture it. So, if only three cannonballs, or maybe none, were fired, what was the likelihood that one of them would have been found and put up for sale, which I learned to be the case about 1999?

A little caveat research by the prospective emptor, me, revealed, however, that in a short cavalry and artillery duel the day before the battle, in the same area, a shot from one of the Twin Sisters struck the Golden Standard's limber and scattered some of its ordnance. It was possible, then, that one or more cannonballs had been left on the field for possible recovery at a later time.

Not being quite as callow as I'd been in earlier years, I decided to contact the seller and ask to look at it, talk about its recovery, and find out all I could before making a financial investment. When I did, I was told that it was part of a large collection that had been amassed by a man who was now elderly, who had collected Texana for decades, and that all of it was now for sale. It was being handled by a young man hired for the purpose of selling off the collection by commission, and he scheduled an appointment for me to come see everything the old collector had for sale.

The collection was stored in what had once been an automotive service station located in a part of Houston that was, shall we say, not River Oaks. The owner/collector was on site, but he seemed standoffish and uncommunicative and let his young salesperson do all the talking. Maybe he was mournful about selling off his prizes. Maybe he didn't want to be asked embarrassing questions.

Inside the three or four rooms that had once been an office and service bays were boxes and boxes of artifacts of all description. I was told I could poke around all I liked and that all was for sale. Included with military relics were numerous crucifixes and religious symbols that supposedly came from Spanish missions and early town sites. I asked if there were any other San Jacinto items, and there turned out to be two cannon balls and, I was told, numerous Mexican army buttons and insignia. I was shown a single Mexican button, which was damaged, with a dark brown patina and a fusilier-type flaming bomb symbol on its face but was told that it and the other Mexican army artifacts, despite what was said earlier, were not then for sale.

I was a little experienced in what brass and other metal artifacts look like when they come out of the ground after being buried for years and years, and as far as I could tell, the items looked okay. Still, it isn't hard to fake a patina, add some dirt, dust, and rust, and thereby age a modern item.

There was, however, a story that went with the two cannonballs, like dinner and a show.

They were recovered, it seems, from the site of the Battle of San Jacinto several years earlier, with landowner permission, from a place in private property located not far from the San Jacinto monument. In fact, the place from where they were excavated, I was told, was the *real* site of the battle, not that other spot with the great big Washington Monument–type thingy sticking up on it.

According to the collector/owner, as translated by the young salesperson, the State of Texas was given the land where the San Jacinto monument is now located, many years ago. It is near the battlefield, but it just isn't the main part of the battlefield. The main battle was fought several hundred yards away, but the fiscally frugal former fathers of Texas decided to go ahead and put up the monument on the land that had been given the state rather than get picky and technical about precise historic locations, which would certainly cost more money.

As proof, sort of, the young salesman exhibited a newspaper clipping from a Houston paper from a few years previous in which the collector/owner's claim was, if not substantiated, at least given some publicity. As further proof I was told that while relic hunting on the private land, the collector/owner had unearthed the original marker placed a few years after the battle at the site where Sam Houston was wounded (probably by a shot from one of his own men). There is a similar, modern marker for the site of Houston's wounding on the battlefield near the monument that is, I was told, not in the right place.

Seemed pretty far-fetched to me, then and now. As for the cannonballs, one was a typical iron ball that would have been consistent with a twelve-pounder. The other was misshapen, possibly made of copper, and looked to me to be too large for a six-pound Twin Sister and too small for the Golden Standard. Having made the trip, however, I decided to put some more of my money on a square of the big roulette game of historical artifacts and took the larger ball home with me. It even included, you guessed it, a certificate of authenticity.

Maybe, just maybe, the old fellow's story will get some more coverage someday. Maybe my investment will be redeemed, and I will discover I am more unscrewed than I suspect I am, but I'm not holding my breath.

Before I tell you about one more item in my little collection, lest its story and those preceding it cause you to decide I habitually wear a "Kick Me" sign taped to my back when it comes to artifacts, let me assert that I have and still own various items of unimpeachable authenticity. Ninety-nine out of a hundred, or better, of all the items I've acquired in the last thirty-five years are above reproach, lots of which are simply too common and inexpensive to be anything else. When I discover that an item is of dubious lineage, I cull it out of my collection, at a financial loss, and tell its next owner what I once believed and what I've learned about it since. Otherwise I couldn't sleep nights and might have folks write nasty things in my visitors log if I ever have one. This next item, however, is bound to cause folks to raise their eyebrows and shake their heads in a knowing manner.

I've mentioned the world's largest flea market, eBay, and while it carries loads of items of questionable parentage and character, it also offers some rare finds. It should be added that it has done wonders for the ability of novice collectors to acquire items at reasonable prices.

The price tag on relics, during the three and a half decades I've collected them, has climbed steadily. A Confederate belt plate that sold for $1,000 in 1975 might fetch $4,000 to $8,000 today. Standard issue 1860-model light cavalry sabers used to be available for $75 to $100 apiece and now are hard to find for less than $300. Furthermore, events that captured the public's imagination intermittently caused relic prices to soar and spike.

Ken Burn's marvelous documentary, *The Civil War*, as well as the movie *Glory*, plus the 125th anniversary of the war and its attendant re-enactments of epic proportion all conspired to send relic prices soaring. That would have been great if I was a seller, but for the most part I'm a buyer. EBay, on the other hand, has revealed the magnitude of available Civil War relics and has made prices a little more reasonable. Goodo.

So it was that I began perusing eBay on a regular basis for bargains or items of particular charm, and occasionally I would decide that I wanted to add a certain type of item that I had never owned to my collection and would begin a regular search for it.

I've always been fascinated by flags. As a boy I charged over many a terraced pasture waving a worn bath towel on a broken well rod as my regimental colors. I was even known, at age thirteen or fourteen, to mount my gelding, Pecos, in full Confederate uniform and, bearing a starred battle flag, to race trains that passed by the railroad tracks that ran a half mile or so from my parents' home in the Panhandle, to the quizzical amusement of the railroad employees.

Confederate flags, however, were completely off the chart of my budget and were a favorite of fakers, as well as not being an item of even remote political correctness. I decided instead, around 2000, to find and purchase a U.S. flag from the Civil War period.

They were still affordable, so long as one wasn't looking for one with genuine military history. I had owned one once before that was huge, eight feet by twelve, and practically impossible to display, so I decided to try and find one with thirty-three to thirty-five stars that was small enough to fit in a frame, perhaps no larger than two feet by three feet. That meant it would be nothing more than a sort of patriotic civilian item, not much larger than the little flags folks wave these days in parades or use to decorate soldiers' graves on Memorial Day.

A fairly steady stream of original Civil War period flags showed up on eBay, at least one a month, but many were too large or too small and most were too expensive. On the rare occasion that I bid on one, I was either unsuccessful winning it or the price escalated out of range.

One day I found one the right size and age, two foot by three, sporting thirty-four stars, which made it of 1861 to 1863 vintage. It was not in great shape, being of silk, wrinkled and rather ragged in places, but it had one other feature. It came with a history and an old-looking handwritten note that said, "This is one of the little flags that was draped over the coffin of Abraham Lincoln."

Yeah, right, of course it was.

I questioned the seller. His story was as follows: The flag had been found in a trunk in a house that once belonged to Brigadier General Charles Cleveland Dodge. The trunk had reportedly been left behind when the Dodge home in Sangerfield, New York, was sold by the family. A subsequent owner found it and kept it until moving to Florida to retire, at which time he sold the trunk and its contents to the current owner, who was not particularly a collector of Civil War relics and who was selling the flag, a carte de visite photo of U.S. Grant, and a handful of other items that were in the trunk.

Silk, thirty-four-star flag found among the personal effects of Federal Brigadier General Charles Cleveland Dodge of New York City. Image owned by author.

The seller seemed straightforward, or perhaps I wanted him to seem so, and didn't place a lot of emphasis on the Lincoln connection one way or another. He only claimed to know what accompanied the flag when he acquired it but said he would toss in a paper item or two that had Dodge's name on it from the trunk to whoever purchased the flag.

Quick research revealed that Dodge was an exceptionally young Federal officer from New York City who commanded a unit of cavalry in Virginia. He was involved in an engagement at Norfolk in January 1862 and another in Suffolk, North Carolina, but he had not seen a lot of action otherwise. He was promoted to brigadier general in November of that year, at the age of twenty-one, but resigned the following June and returned to New York after getting into a snit with his commanding officers, who wanted someone older to command their cavalry, despite the fact that Dodge had a decent record.

Back in the city, he assisted in putting down the draft riots that occurred there in mid-July. He was the son of a former congressman, William Earl

Dodge, a Wall Street financier during the war. The younger Dodge remained in New York for the rest of his life, serving as a partner in a company called Phelps and Dodge and later as president of Boston Cape Cod Canal Company. He died in 1909.

I decided to ignore the possible Lincoln connection and to bid on the flag only to the extent that it was what I was originally seeking—a smallish flag of the right time period that could be framed. To my surprise, I won it for a decent price.

The seller threw in a business card of Dodge's and an envelope with his name on it, and I began to research the Lincoln connection. I also had the flag archivally mounted and framed by a specialist in historic cloth restoration and preservation and had it appraised. To my satisfaction, it was identified as genuine for the period and was valued at well in excess of what I had paid for it, again without the Lincoln connection being critical to its provenance.

In addition to the handwritten note, 3" × 4.5" in size, written in old-fashioned cursive and browning ink, it came with the lid of a deteriorating white cardboard box on which the same, fading description had once been written in pencil.

But I could find no record of anyone placing or draping little flags over Lincoln's coffin. I thought that perhaps a mourner, maybe Dodge, had laid the flag on the casket as he or she passed by, as a souvenir, but there was no available record of that having occurred. I contacted two different authors of books about Lincoln's assassination and his funerals, but they could only attest to there having been one large flag draped over the coffin while it was on the train that carried his body home to Springfield, Illinois, and to flowers being placed on the coffin at certain times and locations—no little flags. It is worth noting that when Lincoln's body was exhumed in 1901 for reburial in its permanent tomb, the casket was opened and the body was viewed by twenty-three people who noted the remnants of what appeared to be a small U.S. flag on the president's chest.

Lincoln did not have just one funeral. Following one in Washington, D.C., on April 18 (he died on the 15th), his body and that of his son Willie, who had died in 1862, were placed on a train that carried them 1,654 miles to Springfield. Along the way, the train stopped numerous times, and massive services were conducted in numerous cities, including Philadelphia, New

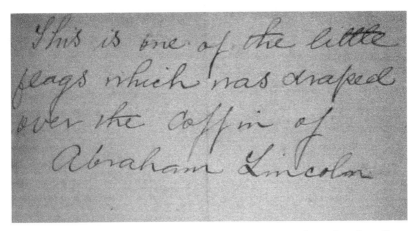

Handwritten note that accompanied the Dodge flag. The remains of a small cardboard box found with the flag bore the same statement. Image owned by author.

York City, Buffalo, Cleveland, and Columbus. In some cities the casket was removed and mourners were allowed to pass by and view the body where it was laid on specially constructed biers. In others the train merely remained in the station while mourners paid their respects from outside. The train arrived in Springfield and the final service was held on May 3, 1865.

I've attempted to locate the papers of General Dodge but so far without success.[22] I did, however, find a newspaper account describing a committee of representatives from Wall Street who journeyed to Washington, D.C., shortly after the assassination to meet with the new president, Andrew Johnson. One of the committee named in the article was General Dodge's father, and the committee would have been in Washington at or about the time of the first of Lincoln's funerals. It was conceivable that either Dodge accompanied his father to Washington and they attended the funeral there or that the elder Dodge attended the funeral and brought the little flag back to New York with him. At least there was a connection, albeit tenuous.

Unless something showed up in some future newspaper, diary, or letter, it was unlikely that I would ever be certain that the flag was ever within a thousand miles of Lincoln's body. However, after owning if for five or six years and continuing to periodically poke about for clues, I found what I now consider to be the best possibility for certifying the Lincoln connection.

One of the better known of the funerals was that in New York City,

An engraving from *Harpers Weekly* newspaper of May 6, 1865, depicting the viewing of Lincoln's body in New York City on April 25, 1865. Note the small U.S. flags at the corners of the top of the catafalque, which are furled, or "draped over the coffin." Courtesy of *Harpers Weekly*.

because it was there that the only surviving photo in which Lincoln's body can be seen was taken. There were other photos taken, but Secretary of War Stanton ordered them destroyed. One escaped detection, however, and came to light in 1952 when a fifteen-year-old student of Lincoln found it among the papers of John Nicolay, Lincoln's private secretary, in the Illinois State Historical Library.

The photo shows the casket on its bier in the New York City Hall, flanked by an admiral at its head and a general at its foot, with busts of famous personages behind and heavy drapes above and further back but no flags. General Dodge might have attended that particular service, I thought, as it was in his home town, but I had no clue to believe it to be so.

Then I stumbled across another image of the casket on its bier. This one was an engraving, and it depicted the entire structure. At the top, arranged in four sets of four to six each, were small U.S. flags furled or draped as decoration.

Might it be possible that after the ceremony, as the platform and bier were being dismantled, that those little flags, some of which probably had thirty-four stars and others thirty-five, were distributed to persons of renown who were in attendance or that at least one of them was given to former Brigadier General Dodge?

Could be. Who knows? Close as I may come to knowing.

12

Pretending on Stage, in Stages

On no other stage are the scenes shifted with a swiftness
so like magic as on the great stage of history. . . .

EDWARD BELLAMY

Looking Backward, author's postscript (1888)

IN 1980 A GROUP OF CITIZENS OF FAIRFIELD, TEXAS, DECIDED TO
form a theater group. They decided to call themselves the County Seat
Players, based on Fairfield being the county seat of Freestone County, got
some funding from the local chamber of commerce, and demonstrated
their appreciation by performing a one-act slapstick comedy titled *Hanging
at Sinimin City* at the chamber's annual banquet that March. It was popular
enough to be performed again the following August at the equivalent of the
county fair, which was called the Annual Reunion in Fairfield because it was
an outgrowth of reunions of the United Confederate Veterans that were
held each year for several decades during the last part of the nineteenth and
first third of the twentieth centuries.

The next summer they performed again, selecting a "western melodrama" called *The Saga of Sagebrush Sal,* which included songs, dances, and a

large cast. The next year, 1982, the group decided to be more ambitious and to perform a three-act murder mystery/comedy, *Bull in a China Shop*.

The players in the little group of amateur thespians ranged in age from just out of high school to retirement, and when they divided up the roles, they discovered that all but one was easy to fill. That one role was the main part, more or less. At least it was that of the person most likely to be voted the bull had there been an election in the china shop. It was for a character named Dennis O'Finn described in the script as a handsome Irish detective. His function was to serve both as the narrator of the play, its crime solver, and as the target of the affections of a group of elderly ladies who, it turned out, were committing murders solely for the purpose of getting him to come spend time with them.

I've never been accused of being handsome, but I was new in town, having been hired the previous summer to work there for the Dow Chemical Company in a lignite project it had launched in the mid-1970s. Having a new lawyer move to a town of less than 5,000 inhabitants was a matter of great local interest, almost exotic, particularly because my wife was also an attorney and had opened a private practice in Fairfield as the only female lawyer in three counties. Furthermore, it was the general consensus and expectation that Dow was going to turn a lot of the citizens of Fairfield and the surrounding area into millionaires, which added incentive to ask me to try out for the role of Detective O'Finn.

The reason Dow Chemical was expected to make millionaires out of locals was because Dow was buying and leasing up thousands of acres of land in several counties, most particularly Freestone County, for lignite. Lignite is a soft brown coal that is plentiful in Texas, particularly in the Wilcox geologic formation that runs diagonally from southwest to northeast like a bandolier. The lignite is most plentiful and closest to the surface in the east and northeast parts of the state, as well as Louisiana. It must be removed by strip mining to a depth of 200 feet, which means everything on top of the ground where it is located must be destroyed or removed. It has a high sulfur content, and when burned produces more pollution than do bituminous and anthracite coal and at lower BTU levels. Nevertheless, it had been the source of power in some electric-generating plants in Texas since as early as 1926, and enough of it exists to supply a lot of energy for a lot of years.

Dow was not in the lignite business for fun or profit or because it was competing to retain a reputation for environmental destruction. It was in the business because it was legally required, under energy and environmental federal laws enacted during the 1970s, to convert to an alternative fuel source to supply its huge petrochemical plants located on the Texas coast. Dow and several other large corporations, such as Alcoa, Shell, and Tenneco, had responded to the new laws by rushing into eastern Texas and western Louisiana with bundles of cash and strong motivation to convince landowners that it would be okay to have their property literally turned upside down. Dow put together the largest bundle of cash, offered the highest royalties, and was able to put together huge holdings of the fuel, in the ground at least, in a relatively short period of time.

The landowners who leased their land to Dow made a handsome profit by doing so and were paid handsomely each year in "advance royalties" that would be subtracted from the actual royalties earned when the lignite was ultimately mined. What the landowners did not know, however, was how much lignite was located on their particular parcels of land and when it would be mined.

The depth and thickness of each vein of the coal was known to Dow, of course, and only Dow's management knew when and where it intended to initiate actual surface mining. The lignite leases were long-term, being for twenty-five to fifty years in duration and held alive thereafter by production if land covered by a lease was included in a working mine when it expired.

Some of the landowners were not so long-term, however. They had made some serious money by leasing their land to Dow, but in most cases they wanted to haul in the rest of the fortune that the lignite lease promised while they were still young enough to enjoy it. More than a few of them were impatient to get the lignite and the royalties flowing. Probably the hottest topic in the coffee shops of Fairfield throughout the 1970s and early 1980s involved speculation and rumors about Dow's plans. Many a scheme was hatched that involved speculative purchases of land Dow might go after in the future, holding out for more money on land Dow had already tried to lease or purchase, and various plots and subplots that culminated in the plotters' minds with large chunks of Dow revenue flowing out of the company's coffers and into those of Freestone County natives. Perhaps the best source of information that might guide, or at least fuel, such speculation might come from the people who worked for Dow, if they were willing to talk.

I was hired in 1981 to work as an attorney in Dow's lignite headquarters in Fairfield as part of its acquisition and title curative team. My previous job, which was my first after law school, had been with the state's water rights, water quality, and water development agency, which is now the Texas Commission on Environmental Quality. After nearly five years working for the state, I'd decided to move on partly for career reasons but particularly because I needed to do so in order to marry Patty/Pat/Ramrod.

While working for the state agency, I'd been made supervisor of an eight-lawyer legal section, and in 1979 two of the attorneys took jobs elsewhere. We posted their positions and began interviewing to replace them. One of the first applicants was an attractive young lady who had just taken the bar exam but would not receive her test results for another three or four months, so she could not be considered for the jobs. The approach to interviewing job applicants that I believed worked best was to have all of the attorneys in the section meet and talk with all the candidates and to then decide by majority vote who to hire. In addition to the normal importance of teamwork and compatibility, our legal section was required to work closely with each other on a large number of adjudicatory hearings, and we'd proved to be most effective when we had a minimum of personality clashes and intra-office politics.

We were a diverse group, with African American, Hispanic, and female representation in addition to white males, but we were all about the same age and we shared the same general attitude about life and politics, fancying ourselves as young Turk activists in regard to water rights and environmental regulation. In other words, we were exactly the kind of young attorneys who were destined to set on edge the teeth of most of the industries we regulated and the attorneys who represented them.

Three things happened near the end of the interviewing process. First, our group met, discussed the candidates we'd talked with so far and agreed that the two we liked best were George and Jim. Second, a day or two after that meeting another candidate, who was an African American lady, interviewed with us. Third, a day or two after that, another of our little team of attorneys announced that she was going to take a different job.

A high level of turnover among lawyers who work for the state was and still is normal. State agencies employ lots of attorneys but cannot afford to pay them a lot. The agencies provide great training in the areas over which they have jurisdiction but four to six years of such training is about all a young lawyer with requisite skills and snap should expect or want to endure before either taking a job in private practice or moving up the ladder to a position of greater responsibility. All of the attorneys in the section I supervised had plenty of skill and snap, and thus it was hard to keep a full team together for more than a few months at a time.

A few days after receiving the news that we would have yet another lawyer job vacancy to fill, the young black lady who had interviewed for the first two jobs called me to ask about the status of our hiring. Thinking I would be giving her good news, I said something like, "When you came in to interview we had pretty much made our minds up about who we were going to hire, but now we have another opening, so if you would like to be considered for that one, we will do so." What I intended as upbeat, she heard as "you applied for and interviewed for a job, but we didn't really consider you for it." The next day she filed an EEOC complaint.

My boss, the general counsel, gave me the good news and said that the executive director of the agency wanted to talk to us about it. Yippee.

The executive director of the agency at that time was a large potato of a man with an impressive beak for a nose and a pompadour hairstyle that might withstand a hurricane. He had a marked southern accent, a good-old-boy attitude, and a booming voice. He was known, secretly and not too affectionately, among his legal staff as "Foghorn Leghorn."

The general counsel was his opposite, a thin, balding, bearded intellectual young man who loved to discuss esoteric legal theories and the status of the latest contested cases being handled by his lawyers. He and the executive director despised each other.

Mr. Leghorn had us ushered into his office, and I delivered my explanation about what had happened. I did not get in trouble in the least. Both he and the general counsel knew me and understood that I had not intended the "already made up our minds about who to hire" comment as it was taken. The big man nodded his understanding and directed us to "start all over again," post all three job openings, and go through the interviewing process from the beginning.

He did not say "hire the black lady," nor did it occur to me, the general counsel, or any of the lawyers who participated in the next round of interviews that we were expected to hire her. However, after a couple of weeks and discussions with several candidates, we got together and decided to offer the jobs to Jim, George, and her.

I delivered the news to the general counsel, who was mildly surprised, but he said he would report our decision to the head office and would let us know when we could officially deliver the offers to the three lucky job applicants. Normally this latter step consisted only of having the human resources department do some routine background checks, confirm pay scales, and set up the necessary files and paperwork. Several days went by, however, and I heard nothing back. Then the general counsel informed me that the two of us had been summoned to the executive director's office again.

We appeared, not knowing the purpose of the meeting but feeling no apprehension. The expression on Foghorn's face, however, and the first words out of his mouth, convinced us that we should.

"You think you're pretty damned smart, doncha?" he said.

The general counsel and I exchanged confused glances.

"You think you got me just where you want me, doncha?" he continued.

We stammered something, probably a polite equivalent of, "WTF are you talking about?"

"I know how you all feel about me," he continued, "and I see right through your little scheme. You come in here and recommend that I hire this proven trouble-maker, and what is going to happen if I don't? She's going to file another EEOC complaint against me is what is going to happen. She's going to find out that you wanted to hire her but that I wouldn't do it, and then it's going to be my ass that is on the line, while y'all just sit back and laugh. Oh yeah, you really think you got me over a barrel this time, but you don't."

He cocked an eyebrow, squinted one eye almost shut, and leveled a hawkish glare at us with the other. "Let me just tell you what we're going to do instead. I believe I'm just going to declare a little hiring freeze in our legal division. We're not going to offer jobs to anyone for awhile. We're going to find out how well you like trying to do your jobs three people short. That's what we're going to do."

Which is what happened. For the next two or three months we struggled to accomplish the work of eight attorneys with five. More critical to resolution of the situation, the general counsel found and took a job in private practice, where he is to this day, and was replaced with an attorney more to the executive director's liking.

After the hiring freeze was lifted, we posted the three job openings, went through another round of job interviews, and ultimately offered the jobs to Jim, George, and to that young lady who had interviewed at the front end of the whole debacle but had not had her bar results and law license at that time; she had received both by then. Her name, in case you didn't see it coming, was Patty, the future Patty/Pat/Ramrod.

I don't know what became of the young African American lady, but after a year or so of working together, Patty and I began dating and then began talking about getting married. That sort of fraternization among coworkers is frowned upon, of course, and the state agency we worked for took it a step further and prohibited persons who were married to each other from working there. Such a rule might not be enforceable now, but it was in 1981.

I was ready to leave the agency anyway, so I began applying for jobs elsewhere and was hired by Dow. This was both a blessing and a curse. It allowed me to leave state employment and change the direction of my career from environmental and water law to energy and mineral law, which looked at the time to be a wise move. More importantly, it would allow Patty and me to be married. Finally, it meant working for a Fortune 500 company that promised top wages and long-term job security.

On the flip side, it meant leaving our beloved Austin to live in a small town on the border of East Texas, and it meant going to work for the company famous for manufacturing Agent Orange, silicone breast implants, and dioxin. Patty cried the first time she saw Fairfield and contemplated having to live there, not because it is an ugly place, but because it was so far from where she wanted to be, live, and practice law. She was an open-minded city girl, and Freestone County was neither progressive in attitude nor urban in setting.

The job, in terms of people and activity, turned out to be fine, but it took me about three years to become comfortable with the idea of working for Dow. When I left Austin, my friends in the city hosted a going-away party, the invitation of which depicted me sitting in the open cockpit of a biplane and sprinkling carcinogenic PCBs onto the countryside below. The "profit first and profit foremost" attitude of the corporation was at odds with my perceived self-image as an altruistic champion of civil rights and the environment.

After a few years, however, I came to understand a truism about the American capitalist system that has stuck with me and that most altruistic champions of civil rights and the environment are denied the opportunity to observe or experience.

Dow employed highly qualified professionals, particularly engineers, and rewarded those who demonstrated the ability to make a profit and/ or to solve problems by promoting them up the corporate ladder. The best and the brightest of these were typically assigned to managerial positions over various company plants and projects around the country. Each manager had a budget for his or her plant or project, of course, that included a slush fund, sometimes of significant size, for the purpose of allowing that manager to pursue innovative ideas for making more money.

There did not seem to be much in the way of restrictions on what a particular manager might decide to do with the money, so long as it was legal and the manager accounted for it. That is, just because Dow was famous for manufacturing chemicals did not mean that the only thing its executives were expected to pursue were ideas involving chemical manufacturing. For example, the project manager of the lignite project in Fairfield learned about the discovery of some igneous rock formations called kimberlites, which are typically a source of industrial diamonds. The kimberlites were not located in Texas but in the far-off Upper Peninsula of Michigan. Nevertheless, the manager theorized that securing the formations might be financially advantageous for Dow, so he dispatched the manager of the land acquisition department in the Fairfield office to the Upper Peninsula, funding the effort from his lignite project slush fund.

This development made me realize that the way capitalism solves problems is by making the solution profitable. Dow did not, as far as I knew, have a particular need or use for industrial diamonds, but it had fair-haired boys who were willing to spend several hundreds of thousands of dollars securing potential kimberlite formations. What might it do if there was money to be made in environmental cleanup, feeding the hungry, or housing the homeless?

The other thing the development did was cause me to be promoted, at least temporarily, into the position previously occupied by the head of the land acquisition department. That, in turn, caused me to take on an extra aura of attraction for the good folks of Freestone County who wanted to be my friend, at least if I was willing to share information with them about the timing and location of Dow's plans to mine lignite. That newfound popularity may, in fact, have had something to do with my being asked to assume the role of the "handsome" Dennis O'Finn, a.k.a. the bull in the china shop.

If that was the case, I was much too naïve to put it all together when the role was offered to me. All I knew was that I was suddenly one of the popular kids that people wanted to see perform. I had been in plays in high school and the "law school follies" at the University of Houston, and so I worked up what I believed was an Irish accent, memorized the lines, attended the rehearsals, and in May 1982 participated in two or three performances of the play in the auditorium of Fairfield High School.

Thereafter I unwittingly became the town jester or village idiot. If the junior high school needed somebody to dress up like Pancho Villa and perform a one-man skit to promote "Reading is Fundamental," Akers was available. If the Rotary Club wanted to put on a magic show, all they had to do was ask, and Akers would learn some card tricks and how to stick a huge needle through a balloon without popping it. When the County Seat Players decided to perform an old-fashioned melodrama filled with corny songs and slapstick humor, Akers was right there to be the Snidely Whiplash kind of villain, kneeling on one knee and belting out a song to the heroine before kidnapping and tying her to the railroad tracks.

By now the question may have been fired from more than one reader's "what does this have to do with" synapse to his or her "trash history" synapse, but just as it was necessary to visit the filming of *North/South* in order to learn about what might have been Custer's gauntlets, there is a connection.

Which is that when a gentleman who grew up in Mexia, Texas, and went on to become a director on Broadway returned to his old hometown with the idea of celebrating the 100-year anniversary of the founding of Camp Joseph E. Johnston by getting someone to perform a one-man play about it, he was told that Akers was the fool to go to.

It was previously mentioned, in connection with the first play the local theater group performed, that there was an annual county fair–like event in Fairfield called the Annual Reunion, a historic leftover from the days when local Confederate veterans got together each year. In Fairfield that reunion was held at the "Reunion Grounds," which looked exactly like the area called the fairgrounds in most towns, except that the Fairfield version included a large number of what appeared to be stalls, perhaps for the purpose of selling concessions or displaying the homemade pies and cakes, homegrown vegetables, and farm animals that are a staple of county fairs. That was not the purpose of the stalls at all.

Each of them, and there were more than fifty, was a "camp" that was once occupied by a Confederate veteran and his family. The annual reunions of the veterans throughout the South began in the late 1880s or early 1990s and continued until the veterans finally died off in the 1930s and 1940s. It was *the* social event of the year, not only in Freestone County but in numerous southern cities and counties.

When they began, the reunions were similar to gatherings of other veterans or of fraternities, sororities, high school classes, summer camp counselors, retirees from large companies, or any other group that was once close, within which friendships were formed but that time and circumstances have pulled apart. That is, they were an opportunity for the old friends to get together, reminisce, tell tales, have a laugh or a cry, and share memories. As the years went by and the reunions became more entrenched and traditional, they grew into something larger and more significant. They were accompanied by speeches, music, dances, plays, skits, visits by dignitaries, concessions, displays, dedications, songfests, beauty pageants, and political campaigning. Not just the veterans, but their families, friends, and distant relatives attended. What started as a one- or two-day event over a weekend became week-long celebration. Families came to town in wagons stocked with provisions, set up housekeeping in their respective camps, and settled in for the duration.

The camps were not literally owned by each family, but the location of each was claimed or assigned to a family, at least for so long as their veteran patriarch was able to attend, and everyone knew whose camp was whose. Some people took pride in constructing elaborate entrances, flooring, and rail perimeters for their camps. Others just marked off an area, threw bedding on the ground, built a fire, and emulated the camping habits of Confederate soldiers. This annual reunion tradition became entrenched in Fairfield and in towns throughout the South and remained so for about half a century.

By the time Patty and I moved to Fairfield in 1981, the veterans were long gone and the tradition of the annual reunion being a notable social event was mostly a thing of the past. It was still called the annual reunion, but it lasted only a weekend, had all the characteristics of a county fair, and demonstrated no obvious connection to the War Between the States. Families no longer occupied the camps for significant periods of time, although they might set up lawn chairs and an outdoor grill in a manner similar to people who "tailgate" before a college football game today.

Nevertheless, the old camps were still considered to be the "property" of whatever family had occupied them in earlier days, and woe be it unto him or her who suggested otherwise. Patty found that out the hard way. She became the city attorney of Fairfield and once came up with the bright idea, in connection with beautifying the city, of tearing down the odd, mismatched, ramshackle collection of pens that were jumbled together in the park on the east side of town. She might have received more support if she had proposed initiating ritualistic cannibalism.

Camp Joseph E. Johnston was Limestone County's equivalent of Fairfield's Reunion Grounds. However, whereas the veterans of Freestone County limited their efforts to holding an annual reunion, those in Limestone County decided that they wanted a beautiful site in which to get together.

The camp is situated in a shady grove near a live creek a few miles away from the nearest town, Mexia. There is a large, arched, metal gate at the entrance with the name of the camp along the top. In the center is a large, gazebo-like pavilion, big enough to host an orchestra, a play, or a ballroom dance. Two old log cabins from other locations in the county have been placed on one side of the area and restored, and on the other side of the camp is another arched entrance to a trail that follows the meanders of the creek and is called "Flirtation Walk." Old signs from the Victorian years when they were erected, advertising sarsaparilla, lemonade, and "hokey pokey" (ice cream) for sale, have been preserved or restored. The camp or park exudes charm and makes a visitor feel as though he or she has stepped into the 1890s.

Next to the pavilion is one of the two surviving "Val Verde Cannons," which is a three-inch rifled gun that was captured by Confederates during the Val Verde campaign in New Mexico in 1862, utilized in a battery of artillery throughout the rest of the war, and, rather than be surrendered in 1865, was buried, along with its twin, in a carriage house near the old settlement of Steward's Mill in Freestone County. The two guns remained there until Grover Cleveland was elected president in 1884. His being a Democrat convinced the locals that not only was Reconstruction over but that it must be okay to be seen in the company of artillery in a southern state again, so the two guns were disinterred. One of them currently graces the front lawn of the county courthouse in Fairfield, while the other is at Camp Joseph E. Johnston.

The Broadway director, whose name I'll leave out for reasons that will become clear later, grew up on land that bordered Camp Joseph E. Johnston. He was in his sixties or early seventies when I met him, and he had attended the reunions at the camp while the veterans were still alive and lively. He told me about people driving wagons, carriages, and early automobiles to the camp and staying there for a week, listening to speeches and symphonies, dancing, visiting, picnicking, and, in some cases, refighting the Civil War. Despite a heady career on Broadway, his success at which was marked by numerous awards, plaques, and mementos on display in his home and related to plays he had directed, the old reunions at Camp Joseph E. Johnston remained among his fondest memories.

So when he decided to direct another play, the idea for which was his own conception, and began casting about for a likely performer, I was targeted. Why not?

By then, 1988, the County Seat Players had fallen into dysfunction. It had not been able to pull together enough interest for production of another performance since 1984. In fact, I had served as its last chairperson, or director, somewhat unwillingly, and the headaches of selecting a play, rounding up volunteers to commit, rehearse, and perform, scheduling rehearsals and performances, and all the other responsibilities of the job totally eclipsed the glamour of the office.

I also had become distracted by other developments. I'd become a father, first in January 1984 and again in December 1985. Then in late 1987 and early 1988 I had run for political office. A group of citizens in Freestone and Limestone counties had convinced me to run for district judge against a ten-year incumbent who had managed to outrage a sizeable number of them. None of the members of the local bar were willing to oppose him, but it had become obvious to me that the Dow lignite project was gradually shutting down and that I needed another career change. The law under which Dow had a deadline to convert to an alternative fuel source had been repealed, lignite mining had never commenced and did not look likely to commence in the foreseeable future, and the company was gradually reducing the size of the workforce in the county, even to the extent of making me the local project manager. I'd been offered jobs with Dow legal divisions in both Midland, Michigan, and Houston but had no desire to move to either city, so I was essentially riding the project into whatever oblivion lay in store for it. The idea of being a judge had appeal, so I agreed to run.

There followed a six-month political slugfest, punctuated by a lot of speeches, attendance at cake sales, visits to churches in black communities, door-to-door solicitations, live and radio candidate debates, and various entertaining, semi-entertaining, embarrassing, and inspiring developments. I was supported by a grassroots movement of hundreds of dedicated people who sincerely wanted the incumbent removed from the bench, led by a tremendously charismatic man who had once been a candidate for the United States Senate.

On election night, out of a total of more than 11,000 votes cast, the incumbent was declared the winner by one vote. I asked for a recount and was declared the winner by three votes.

That led, of course, to an election contest, which went to trial six weeks later. The interim was filled with tracking down and learning the nature of every illegal or suspected illegal vote in two counties, and on the day the trial began in the Freestone County Courthouse in Fairfield, I arrived convinced that of the slightly more than forty votes by nonresidents, underage teen-agers, convicted felons, and folks who voted more than once, more than thirty of them had been cast for the incumbent. I was going to win the election contest and become a district judge.

As Chief Dan George, playing Old Lodge Skins in *Little Big Man,* said, however, "sometimes grass don't grow, the wind don't blow, and the sky ain't blue."

The first few witnesses for the challenger presented the story we expected, and I made a mental note that gave him about the number of votes we'd counted, not more than two or three. Then it switched to our turn, and I learned the alarming news that some of the voters we had subpoenaed to appear were not present. Some had gone on vacation. One had checked into a hospital for elective surgery. What? They had to answer a subpoena, didn't they? Surely they wouldn't refuse to appear when I summoned them just because, uh, they voted for my opponent . . . would they?

Not to worry. We still had plenty of illegal votes to prove up, and my attorney presented the testimony of three, bam bam bam. On the fourth, the attorney for the incumbent objected, saying that this particular vote should have been challenged at the polling place and that it was now too late to do so. I chuckled to myself. What a stupid objection.

The judge sustained it. Suddenly about twenty votes—all similar in theory to the one against whom the objection had just been sustained and that we had intended to prove up as illegal, all for my opponent—vanished from my mental score card.

The next day the other side was allowed to present a new witness. It was a young black lady who had campaigned for me in the community in which she lived, and she approached our table to tell us that my opponent had subpoenaed her father to testify but that he was partially paralyzed and bedfast. She, his granddaughter, knew how he had voted and had come to the courthouse to see if it would be okay if she testified in his place.

We could have objected, of course, but all that would have accomplished would have been that the court would allow everyone to take a field trip to her grandfather's bedroom so that he could answer the questions. My lawyer and I graciously, and stupidly, agreed to let the young lady testify.

On the stand she described how she had helped her grandfather complete an application for a ballot by mail, so that he could vote absentee. The critical nature of her testimony was she revealed that rather than use the affidavit form that was required for an absentee voter unable to sign his or her own name, the girl had simply signed his name for him. Yes, Granddad had directed her to, "Just sign that for me, honey," and she'd merely obeyed, but doing so disqualified the vote.

Not to worry; just one vote.

"And did you do the same thing for anyone else you assisted when you were campaigning for Mr. Akers?" my opponent's attorney asked.

"Well, grandma, and mamma . . ." and nine others.

"And do you know of anyone else who worked in Mr. Akers' campaign who did the same thing?"

"Well, my friend Mae."

"And where is she?"

"Right there in the audience, watching."

Mae was called to the stand and provided verbal proof regarding three more votes for which she had signed, or forged in the eyes of the law, the voters' signatures. At the end of the day my mental scorecard put the count at three votes for my opponent that had been discredited, and sixteen that had voted for me.

The next day we put a man on the witness stand who worked as a handyman for an attorney in Mexia and had been a major supporter of my opponent. The man testified that he had been paid fifty dollars to go down to the "skid row" part of town, round up "bums and homeless people," and drive them to the polls to cast their votes.

Under Texas law in 1988, it was illegal to pay someone to drive voters to the polls. It was an archaic law and has since been repealed, but it suggested that my opponent had been trading drinks for votes, and the newspapers, radio stations, and television station who had reporters covering the event loved reporting about it. It made my opponent squirm but did nothing to change the vote count.

At the end of the third day, a Thursday, the visiting judge presiding over the election contest announced that court would recess until Monday, at which time each side should have drafted and submitted a brief arguing the meaning of the evidence and its legal impact. My attorney was a capable trial attorney from Mexia who despised the incumbent and who was handling my case pro bono. He was devoted to the cause of getting him off the bench but not so much so that he was going to sacrifice a three-day weekend writing a brief. He informed me I could do it.

He also proposed that we make my opponent a settlement offer. We could, he suggested, agree to throw the first election out and to have another election. I scoffed at the idea. What possible motive would the incumbent have to agree to that? He was going to win the election contest and be reelected to the bench. Anyone could see that.

I left the courthouse dejected. In all likelihood the efforts and expense of the hundreds of people who had supported me during the previous six months were all a waste. Defeat was almost certain, and the best outcome I could hope for was another election campaign.

The first one had gotten progressively uglier and uglier, with the two counties in the district about as sharply divided as it was possible to be, and even if I won in a second campaign, I would preside over a jurisdiction in which approximately one out of every two people believed I should not be in office. More intimidating and more immediate was the likelihood of the kind of campaign my opponent would wage if we squared off again.

At the beginning of the campaign I had made it a condition of my agreeing to run that my supporters not sling mud or even make issues out of the various incidents that had caused them to detest my opponent. They had not wanted to agree but had no choice as there was no other licensed attorney in the area willing to run. (Patty, by then, had taken a job in Dallas, and we were taking turns commuting the ninety miles each way each day.) The last time anyone had run against the incumbent, he had not only lost but discovered that he was unable to get a favorable ruling on even the most minor matters in the incumbent's courtroom, and he had finally packed up and moved away.

My strategy may have appeared commendable, and it had been generally effective, but my reasons were not altogether noble. I was a child of the 1960s and the 1970s who had alternatively fancied himself a fraternity man and a hippie, meaning I had a few incidents in my background that were more objectionable than wearing plaids with stripes. None were of a criminal nature, but I felt certain that an enterprising investigator sniffing my back trail could find an interesting tale to relate if he located the right, or wrong, people. I had reasoned at the front end of the campaign that if I didn't clobber my opponent with criticism of his acts of poor judgment in the past, maybe he would not clobber me with mine. It had worked until the tail end of the election, when some of my supporters felt obligated to spill the beans to voters unfamiliar with the most outrageous things the incumbent had done. If there had ever been an unwritten mutual understanding about running clean campaigns, it would not necessarily apply if there was another election.

About an hour after leaving the courthouse, my lawyer called to interrupt my mental lamentations. He reported that he had made the settlement offer, that my opponent had considered it and called back to say that he would agree to it . . . on one condition—that we both withdraw from the race and throw our mutual support to the sitting county judge, who we both knew and liked and who had stayed neutral in the previous campaign.

We speculated thereafter and it was hinted that my opponent had reasoned that despite the apparent change in vote count, the most likely outcome of the election contest would be that the judge would order another election. It was simply too close and sentiments were too strong to declare a winner based on the kind of irregularities and technicalities that had been presented in the courtroom. That would mean, the incumbent supposedly believed, that I would probably win the second election. I had proven that he was vulnerable and had done so in a manner that some people considered an appropriate, clean campaign. If that happened and he was defeated by the voters, he would not be eligible to serve as a visiting judge in other counties in the state, particularly Harris County, where Houston is located. If, on the other hand, he merely resigned from the office, he could not only serve legally as a visiting judge in the big city, where visiting judges were needed on a regular basis and at a higher level of pay than he was making in Freestone and Limestone counties, but he would not have to stand for election again.

For me the choice was obvious. The folks who had talked me into running would get what they wanted—the incumbent out of office—and I would neither have to endure another, potentially painful election campaign nor would I have to preside over an area in which I could count on not being supported by almost exactly one half of the people with whom I had contact. I jumped on the deal.

The next day the incumbent and I shocked the voters and the news media by first agreeing to a new election, then mutually withdrawing from it and announcing our support for the county judge. At first my supporters were outraged, convinced I had been bought and paid for and that they had been sold down the river by the wily incumbent. After I explained, tearfully and not altogether truthfully, that I had made the deal in order to accomplish their original goal, and they realized the incumbent was really gone, I experienced a wave of sentimental adulation I neither expected nor deserved.

"At first we just wanted to get him out of office, but once we got to know you we wanted you for our judge," was the general message. I received various letters and notes thanking me and saying things about my noble sacrifice I knew not to believe. One lawyer in another county whom

I'd never met but who was no fan of the incumbent sent a letter stating that what I had done was in the best traditions of the State of Texas and the state bar and was what was best for the district and the counties. He enclosed a check for a thousand dollars that not only paid off my remaining campaign debts but was used by my supporters to award a college scholarship in my name the next year.

So, with that kind of drama in my recent past, the prospect of getting up in front of an audience and pretending to be an old Rebel talking about an old Confederate veterans' reunion grounds sounded just about right.

The Mexia-based director's idea for the one-man play was essentially as follows. A fund-raising banquet for the camp, which had been founded in 1888, was already planned. Following the meal, he would announce that the clock was being rolled back to that year, would introduce me, and I would come out on stage in an officer's frock coat with a patch over one eye and a noticeable limp, aided by a cane. I would then speak as though to myself about the absolute foolishness of establishing a camp at which to hold reunions for veterans of that horrible, wasteful, agonizing war that needed to be erased from all memory instead of celebrated. I would speak of various horrors of the war, how wrong it had all been, how wrong-headed the nation had been to allow it to happen, and would then vow to wash my hands of the whole affair, climaxing the soliloquy with an impassioned declaration that "a hundred years from now nobody . . . *nobody* . . . will ever remember that there was once a Camp Joseph E. Johnston!"

It worked. The audience rose and delivered a standing ovation, the only one I have ever had and ever expect to receive.

Up until then my relations with the director had been that of teacher and pupil. He not only outlined the script and helped me rehearse but attempted to teach me methods and actions that he knew were effective from his many years behind the scenes in the Big Apple. These were conducted in the stately Victorian home in Mexia that he had inherited and to which he intended to retire after one or two more seasons on Broadway.

After the performance, he invited me to his home again for a celebratory toast. I went and was stunned when he proposed that I go with him to New York. I could become a star, he promised. I stammered something about being flattered but not really interested, and he pressed the subject, suggesting I could leave my wife and move in with him. I finally understood.

Musicians and thespians Bill and Carla Coleman of Oregon.
Courtesy of Bill and Carla Coleman.

Unless one counts the battle re-enactments described previously, the Camp Joseph E. Johnston performance was the zenith, and conclusion, of my acting career, at least as one who "struts and frets his hour upon the stage." I did have one more brush with thespians, however, in the form of Bill and Carla Coleman, who were mentioned in the story about Jackson and Janie.

As Bobby Horton had put music, vocals, and arrangement to the lyrics of "The Southern Birthright," Bill wound up putting the same to about a dozen sets of my lyrics. Most were released in the company of other songs, both contemporary and original, as collections of Civil War music on CD and cassette, and a few were incorporated into two of the three two-person musical dramas about the Civil War that the Colemans performed for many years and that they still perform on occasion. They are based in Oregon but spent several years touring the country, particularly the deep South, Virginia, and Pennsylvania, spending one summer as the regular performers at the Conflict Theater in Gettysburg.

After one performance of their original musical drama, called *Taps,* they were approached by a park ranger who was employed at the Monocacy National Battlefield Park in Maryland. Monocacy was a battle fought in June 1864, when Confederate General Jubal A. Early, leading the Second Corps of the Army of Northern Virginia, Stonewall Jackson's old command, attempted to duplicate some of Jackson's military feats in the Shenandoah Valley. Early was initially successful, leading his little army to within rifle range of Washington, D.C., and luring President Lincoln to the ramparts to observe, but Early was forced to retreat, was later pursued by Phillip Sheridan, and his "Army of the Valley" was ultimately destroyed as an effective military force.

The park ranger told Bill and Carla about a set of letters with a Monocacy connection. They had been found in a home that was being cleaned out and made ready for sale by the family of a spinster aunt named Matilda Burrows who had died many years before in a little town in Georgia. One of the relatives took a cigarette break and noticed a packet of letters in a trash can tied together with a faded pink ribbon. He opened one and discovered that it was from a Confederate soldier named George Boatwright. They were love letters addressed to Matilda, or Mattie, and chronicled a romance of unusual poignancy.

George met Mattie at a party in Georgia and then wrote to ask if she would be "his correspondent," as nothing gave a soldier in the field more joy than to receive letters from home. Soon, however, it became apparent that George wanted more than letters. He was smitten with the young lady, and a photograph of her from the period made his reasons obvious, for she was quite an attractive young lady.

The letters, some twenty-four or twenty-five in number, spanned the period from March 1863 to June 1864. None of the letters George received from her were extant, but the tone and content of some could be gleaned from George's side of the correspondence. Having seen each other only once, their affection for each other grew and blossomed. On one occasion he was able to get leave and visit her home, but she was not there. On another, after writing to tell her he was going to do it, he deserted, walked over a hundred miles to her home, and once again found her absent. He had arrived before the letter and, upon returning to camp, was arrested and confined to quarters for several months.

Whatever Mattie wrote, it encouraged George and the tone of his letters became more and more forward. Finally, in the last letter in the collection, he popped the question, saying that she must answer it, for his fate, "for weal or woe," depended on her response—"Will you be my Mattie?"

We do not know how Mattie responded, but within a month George was dead, killed at the battle of Monocacy. Mattie lived out the rest of a long life surrounded by family, but she never married.

I was honored when the Colemans asked me to take the letters and transform them into a play for them to perform. Titled *The Last Rose,* it employs only a modicum of poetic license to weave its sentimental message about love lost and lifelong loyalty of the heart. They have performed it hundreds of times.

13

Genealogy

Great families of yesterday we show, and Lords whose
parents were the Lord knows who.
DANIEL DEFOE
"A True-Born Englishman," 1701

UNLESS SCIENCE DISCOVERS A BIG SURPRISE, THE FAMILY ROOTS OF everyone currently living, as well as everyone who has gone before, can theoretically be traced to the beginning of time. However, unless a person establishes a link with quite a well-known clan or is an extremely diligent Mormon, it is unlikely that he or she will be able to trace further back than a couple or three hundred years, a thousand at the outside.

Some things in life seem intentional, although not many, such as the fact that about one out of a hundred folks in a family, or perhaps one per generation, is passionate about the family's history. That means that whereas the other ninety-nine often have to endure boring lectures, during which their minds stray toward assassination, a record is established that can be passed down to the next singleton family researcher. Mostly, I'm the guy in my clan, although my mother and one of my sisters either care or have been successful disguising their murderous thoughts. I've also been fortunate in running across and acquiring the work of a couple of the ones out of a hundred in other parts of the extended tribe.

These tales were intended as preservation of some incidents associated with American history that I believed should be preserved. They were not intended to be autobiographical in nature, but several of them contain more personal than national history. Discussing one's family tree and expecting a stranger to be interested as opposed to violently repulsed by the prospect seems like the height of conceit. Still, some of the creatures in the Akers family tree lived interesting lives, or lives made interesting, and this may be their only chance to strut and fret on stage again, ever.

A third cousin, who was a doctor but who passed away before I had a chance to meet him, did a lot of research and found one of those mythical links in the family to a family named Bryan that did, in fact, have some very famous folks in it, namely William the Conqueror and his descendants. The first identified grandfather of that line was born in 970, and the descendants included five English kings who are direct ancestors of my siblings and my offspring.

However, before you think I think that is special, consider that it has been estimated that eighty percent of the people currently living in England can trace their lineage directly to King Edward III, who ruled from 1327 to 1377 and had nine children who survived to adulthood. His documented descendants include George Washington, Thomas Jefferson, John Quincy Adams, Zachary Taylor, both Roosevelts; authors Jane Austen, Lord Byron, Alfred Lord Tennyson, and Elizabeth Barrett Browning; Robert E. Lee; Charles Darwin; and actors Humphrey Bogart, Audrey Hepburn, and Brooke Shields. Edward III also happens to be one of the kings in our family line.

Still, while it may be common, it is intriguing to think that royal blood runs in the family's veins and that there is a distant link with so many notables. Admittedly, by the time the bloodline got to the middle of the nineteenth century, the royal nature of it was pretty damned diluted. To be specific, by the time the relevant grandmother, whose name was Agnes Bryan, married into the clan, about 1783, and established the link by which we can now claim all that royal blood, the family she married into, at least in one or more generations, was illiterate. When the 1850 census was taken, one

EDWARD III.

Genealogical research can reveal interesting surprises, such as a direct line to Edward III, King of England from 1327 to 1377, multiple-great grandfather of the author (and millions of others). Reprinted from *Cassell's History of England*.

brother spelled his name Akers while another just a few miles away spelled it Acres. How the mighty can tumble or at least forget how to spell.

According to the third cousin's research, the Bryans witnessed some interesting times and events. Down the line from the ancestors who were monarchs was a knight, Sir Francis Bryan, who served Henry VIII. He lost an eye when his lance "shivered," or splintered, during a joust but was a confidant of the king, and, when Henry needed somewhere to place his daughter by Catherine of Aragon, Mary Tudor, while he busied himself divorcing his queen and establishing the Anglican Church, he chose the mother of Sir Bryan, Lady Margaret Bryan, to raise or at least assist in raising the little girl. The fact that Mary grew up to be Bloody Mary may or may not say something about Lady Bryan's maternal skills.

However, Henry needed to make the same type of arrangement for the baby who would grow up to be Elizabeth I, when it appeared that the baby's mother, Anne Boleyn, was losing her head, and he again chose Lady Bryan. As he had with Mary, Henry lovingly declared the little girl to be a bastard and not in line for the throne. Apparently he did not provide lavishly for the girls either, as an Internet history site notes that "[i]n her young life Elizabeth had a number of governesses, one of whom was Lady Margaret Bryan who had to beg Thomas Cromwell, the king's Chief Minister, for night gowns and chemises for the princess once she grew out of them, clothes that had been ordered by the princess's mother Anne Boleyn.[23]

Sir Francis Bryan was supposedly at the king's side when he died.

A couple or more generations later, an ambitious Bryan grandfather decided to set himself up as the King of Ireland. He engineered an uprising for that purpose, but it failed, and he was exiled to America. His son spent his life trying to regain his father's lands, holdings, and titles, to no avail. If the courts ever decide that descendants of historically mistreated people deserve reparations, my cousins and I might as well claim some vast estates in England. We can figure out which ones if the incentive is ever there to do so.

The man in the family whom Agnes Bryan married was named John Akers. He lived in Campbell County, Virginia, as had the Akers clan since at least the 1750s and possibly the 1730s. He was identified in my cousin's research as "Bunker John" Akers due to the fact that he fought in the Battle of Bunker Hill during the Revolutionary War. I found this fact curious, considering that John would have been only thirteen when the battle was fought and the battle was in Massachusetts rather than Virginia. Still, I repeated the brag several times before discovering that no, while a Bunker John Akers did exist, he was not my thirteen-year-old grandfather.

The real Bunker John was probably a distant relative. Apparently there were three Akers men who arrived in the New World in the 1600s in the area called West Jersey, part of New Jersey today. They went different directions but were probably brothers or otherwise related, with my line settling near what is now Concord, in Campbell County, Virginia.

John may have served in the Revolution, and he certainly served as a militia captain in Campbell County after the war. For the most part, he and his descendants busied themselves trying to coax a living out of the parsimonious soil of southwest Virginia, moving further and further from royalty and closer and closer to illiteracy. A couple of generations after John, a grandfather named George married his own first cousin, which tends to be a bad idea.

The thing that gives marrying one's cousin a bad reputation—generations of wing-nut insanity—either didn't show up in their children or was not diagnosed, but there were problems of some sort before the next generation became a generation, because when George died, in 1851, his widow, Catherine, refused to mourn him. One can assume this meant she refused to wear black and act grief-stricken, but maybe it meant she kicked up her heels and started inviting the young studs of Campbell County over for taffy pulls. Whatever it meant, the rest of the community decided to ostracize her. Even though the family had been there for more than a century, had been founders of the local Presbyterian church, and were intermarried with several of the best families around, like the Dixons.

When the good folks of the region let Grandma know that she was not behaving properly, she simply gave them the finger, figuratively at least, and decided to take her brood west, which she did. Leaving the 300-acre tobacco farm in the care of her oldest son, George Washington Akers, she put the rest of the siblings, including my GGGF, Simon Peter Akers and his family, either on the train or into a wagon train. Family tradition says the latter, but I suspect the former because there was then a train that ran as far west as St. Joseph, Missouri, and the family settled not far from there in Chariton County, near the town of Marceline.

That particular municipality has as its claim to fame today that it served as the model for Main Street USA for Disneyland, but that happened quite a few years after the Akers arrived. The first thing that Grandma, whose name was Catherine, set about to accomplish was establishment of another Presbyterian church, which she did. It took her eight years, but she did it, and when she wrote her sister in Virginia on November 2, 1859, after a long silence, the first sentence and the first page of the four-page letter were about that church. She talked about it before she asked about the new babies, before she reported about her own babes, and before she asked about her mother.

Supposedly the church is still called, to this day, Aunt Catherine's Church.

The letter, being a survivor and a bona fide gold nugget, offers a few other glimpses of life in the clan. She talked about trading locks of hair with family members in Virginia, about being scrawny but in good health, and about getting gray and losing teeth. She mentioned her sister-in-law Mary having her baby baptized and quipped, "her husband is no professor." She mentioned that "Mother lost the girl that brother George brought out," suggesting they owned an occasional slave. The descendants of George still living in Virginia remember a tale of him buying a slave for his wife. The letter ends with something uncharacteristic for the clan—strong verbal affection:

> Oh when will the time arrive when I shall see you and converse with
> you face to face Oh blessed hope my soul leaps up at the thought. Oh
> sister My feelings are almost uncontrollable how I long to embrace you
> in my arms again. God only knows. May he grant it if his will but if
> not may he give me Grace to bear the separating and give us a happy
> meeting beyond the grave is the prayer of your most devoted sister,
> C.E. Akers.

Family tradition is that when the war broke out, my great-grandfather decided to volunteer for the Confederacy and got as far as acquiring and putting on his uniform before his mother and wife decided he should not go. They were strong-minded women, or maybe beta males just run, or skulk, rampant in my line.

That was typical of my genealogical fortune when it came to finding Civil War ancestors. Out of the sixteen family lines that could have produced a soldier in that war, preferably Confederate, Great-Granddad Akers came the closest, which was not close at all. All other men in the ancestral lines, with one exception, were too young, too old, or too something else to serve. The only one out of all the candidates was Great-Great-Grandfather Benjamin Summers, a Missouri hillbilly type on my mother's side, and his war record was about as sparse as one can be and still be considered a war record.

He managed to stay out of either army until John Hunt Morgan made another one of his raids north, his last, and Granddaddy Ben joined the Missouri Enrolled Militia, of Yankee persuasion, for about three months, six at

Genealogical research can also reveal much more humble roots, such as this family portrait, circa 1880, of the Missouri clan of Ben Summers, the author's only direct ancestor who served in the Civil War. Ben is standing inside the corral, right center, visible between the tree and shoulder of the girl standing on the fence. He appears to be holding a young steer by its horns. Image owned by author.

the outside. The extent of his glorious service was told to a great uncle of mine who preserved it and passed it down so that I could be titillated.

Old Ben said that one day their captain was drilling the company and ordered them to practice firing a volley by leveling and blazing away at an old, abandoned cabin in the woods. They fired their volley, which I suspect was ragged in the extreme, and Ben Summers told his nephew that when they did, two men ran out of the back of the cabin and disappeared into the woods, and "they thought they might have been the enemy."

I love that story. It is so anticlimactic that it is classic.

Although there were no direct Akers ancestors in the Civil War, there were plenty of collaterals, including Reuben Cornelius Akers, a first cousin four times removed who served as a cadet at Virginia Military Institute, fought, and was wounded in the Battle of New Market in 1864. His name is on the monument at VMI in Lexington, despite the fact that he subsequently went home on leave and never returned, resulting in his being classified a deserter. He is buried in Lynchburg.

His older brother, Albert Akers, was a captain in the 2nd Tennessee Infantry and was wounded at Shiloh. He survived the war and lived in Washington, D.C. where he and his wife were active in veteran affairs. Mrs. Akers once wrote the *Confederate Veteran* to remark that when the newly elected commander of the Confederate Veterans came to Washington his visit interfered with her opportunity to meet the new U.S. president, Woodrow Wilson, but that "the choice was simple" and she had expressed her apologies to the Wilsons.

I learned about Albert's existence one summer in a trip Patty and the kids and I took to Virginia, where we visited some cousins and were given some genealogical information that the aforementioned third cousin had compiled. The next day, a Thursday, we drove from Campbell County to Washington, where we visited Arlington Cemetery and, therein, the Confederate section.

There is an interesting large monument there depicting people of the Confederacy in larger-than-life bas relief encircling the top portion of the edifice, including soldiers, sailors, ladies, children, politicians, etc. The sculpted people number perhaps forty and are arranged as if following each other in a procession. Near the front of the procession is a man who is obviously an African American. The interesting thing is that he is wearing a Confederate uniform.

After viewing the monument, we turned to leave the Confederate section, in which the graves of veterans are arranged in concentric rings around the monument. Just before we stepped out, Patty said, "Oh look, here's an Akers."

It was Albert. We had found out about him on Wednesday and found him on Thursday. A year or so later we returned in the wake of a Civil War re-enactment, and I had in my possession a reproduction Confederate belt plate that I pressed into the earth at the base of his gravestone, covering it with grass and a few inches of soil. Several years later we returned and ascertained that the belt plate was still there. If it still is but we unwittingly violated some Federal law by placing it there, I hereby disavow all knowledge of what I just wrote.

Coming on down the Akers line a little further, to my own grandfather, the perils of living with strong-minded women become apparent. Catherine's husband, Simon Peter Akers, passed away in 1884, at fifty-seven, from scurvy, thoughtless of how unimpressed his descendants would be about that. He did, however, choose some memorable last words, "I can hear the angels singing," so all was not lost. The older of their two boys was my father's father, Charles, and Great-Grandma C.E. decided when he was a babe he would be a preacher when he was grown.

Perhaps it was an accident or perhaps the streak of gene that took his people out of Virginia and into Missouri struck again, but Granddad foiled C.E.'s plans by swallowing part of a can of lye and wrecking his voice. It was not permanent, it turned out, but it lasted long enough for C.E. to remove her preacher plans from Charlie's shoulders and place them on younger brother Willie Wirt's, and it became so. Willie Wirt grew up to be a Presbyterian preacher and to move back to Virginia and have sons who built a wonderfully successful trucking company that ran up and down the east coast for many years. Granddad's future was stormier.

He married my grandmother, Cleo, in 1895 and moved west for his health soon thereafter, settling on the state border between Texas and the Oklahoma Territory. He owned a livery stable for a while, farmed and ranched, and was a cattle buyer. After selling the livery stable, he bought a ranch of eight sections near Follett, Texas. Eight of the ten children Cleo gave birth to survived, and it looked like a one-to-one land-for-child arrangement was possible until the Panic of 1919. Like many of his countrymen who had overextended their credit, he was wiped out. Unlike most of his countrymen, he was never able to rebuild. Granddad's one great weakness was already too well known in the community for bankers to loan him more money—he drank.

He probably wasn't the first in the line to imbibe, and he wasn't the last, but he may have been the most conspicuous. On one occasion, for example, when his mobility and that of a freight train intersected while he was in his cups, Grandpa rammed the damned thing with his car. He was in plain view, in daylight, and in the middle of a Shattuck, Oklahoma, street that the train was halted across. He warned it. He yelled at it and told it to move, and when it didn't he backed up and charged. That is what I call a thoughtful act. It has entertained generations of family and strangers as well.

His intolerance for liquor was not always humorous, however, for he developed the habit of either brandishing a butcher knife and chasing the family into the pasture at night or going on a burning spree. Sometimes the two events occurred simultaneously, and on more than one occasion Grandma and her brood hid in a field and watched as Granddad carried load after load from the house, piled it high, and set it ablaze.

Grandma received five dollars a month from him to raise eight children, and from that she somehow managed to set aside enough to buy a sewing machine to make clothes for the children. Granddad burned it. On another occasion, learning that Grandma had always longed to have a red dress, a kindly neighbor gave her one for Easter. Granddad burned it. Same with the old antique clock my father loved and a used Sunday bonnet another neighbor gave Cleo.

I heard these tales, though not with much pride, from my parents and also heard that my father, who was the youngest son of the eight, with two younger sisters, would search out and break his father's bottles of booze, which the old man secreted around the ranch. I always assumed that Dad did this when he was a young man or perhaps a teenager. It wasn't until I was grown and my father in his seventies that I learned that no, Dad started doing it at about age six. Nobody asked him to, and nobody urged him to continue, but my father decided it was up to him to take a ball-peen hammer, ferret out my grandfather's stash, and smash it. Dad said he did it many times and that his father never said a word about it. The older Akers just kept hiding, and the younger one just kept searching and smashing. What a fun, creepy game for a kid to play.

Granddad died at the age of seventy-nine and might have lived much longer, at least long enough to capture a longevity record in a short-lived clan, but he had the foresight and concern for his offspring to get killed by a tornado, which is almost as imaginative as getting killed by Indians. In particular, he was rooming with another old gentleman in Higgins, Texas, when he heard what sounded like a freight train outside. It was actually the Tri-State Tornado of April 9, 1947, which killed 181 persons and injured 970. Granddad stuck his head out the window to see what all the noise was, was struck in the forehead by a windblown two-by-four, and became one of the former.

About 1965, the first time I ever visited the Washita battlefield near Cheyenne, carried there by my parents on a Sunday afternoon, we saw the historic site and then went into downtown Cheyenne, what there was of it, so I could see the newspaper office window. I'd read somewhere that after the battle the skeleton of Cheyenne chief Black Kettle was put on display in the window, and even though it was no longer there (and never had been, although another Indian's skeleton may have been) I wanted to see the window. That's the kind of nerd I was and am.

While we were standing on the street near an old building that had a front window and might have once been a newspaper office, my father, Edward, struck up a conversation with a local man. My father did that a lot, never hesitant to find common ground in cattle-market analysis, price-of-wheat news, or just speculation about whether rain was in the offing. In this case the other man asked my father his name and when Dad told him, he said, "You wouldn't be any relation to Charles Akers, would you?" My father said that was his father, and then neither man knew what to say next.

They stood there several long seconds, trying to figure out how to follow up on that bit of information, and finally the other man said something like, "I reckon he was one of those folks you don't realize you're going to miss until after they're gone." My dad nodded his head and said, "Yep."

The colorful folks on my mother's side included three men named Bozier, two brothers and one son, named John, Jonathan, and John. George Foreman would have felt right at home with them. They came to America from France as mercenaries, following Johann De Kalb, to fight in the American Revolution, after which they received land in what became the state of Mississippi, where one of them, almost certainly called John, was killed by Indians.

A great-aunt who raised my mother after her mother was killed in a car accident in 1924, when my mom was eleven, witnessed the Oklahoma Land Rush. Another uncle, in the same extended family, the son of old Ben Summers, married a woman named Amanda Bull, and a family photo that was passed down identifies her in writing on the back as being the daughter of Sitting Bull. Pretty certain that wasn't really the case, I logged into a message board about American Indians and asked if it was so, in response to which I received a complete listing of all of Lakota chief Sitting Bull's offspring and relatives, which included no Amandas. The lady who sent it said, however, that she had seen Amanda Bull's name on a list of false claimants, which has a certain trash-history charm in and to itself. Another man responded by pointing out that there was an Arapahoe chief named Sitting Bull, as well as the more famous Lakota, and that he lived in Oklahoma, as had my aunt by affinity. Perhaps there really is a link, but I've not looked for it any further.

On my wife Patty's side, the family heritage fairly oozes with southern charm and richness. She had more than one Confederate ancestor, including family who were living in Richmond when it fell on April 2, 1865. An aunt married a Captain Walter Bowie, who was a Virginia captain wounded in the foot at Gettysburg and who later served as an inspector of military prisons in the South. He gave the Andersonville Prison Camp a passing grade.

Can you imagine the kind of conversation he and Mrs. Albert Akers might have had?

After the war he managed to get a job at Washington College, after a fellow officer wrote personally to recommend him to its new president, Robert E. Lee. Although his first job was pretty much that of a janitor, he stayed on and rose up the administrative ranks to become a member of the board of trustees. The interesting part of this tale is that he ran errands and did work personally for the Lee family, and he and his wife held on to at least two little notes he received from them which, in turn, were passed down to Patty.

The first, and most legible, is dated June 25, 1869 and says:

Capt. Bowie: Please send one 1 doz chickens & a good roasting piece of
Roast beef, or some other meat instead if you can. Very truly, R.E. Lee.

The other is less legible, in a lighter hand, and is not dated. The penmanship looks very similar to that in the other note, and says,

My dear Mrs. Bowie: Any time that it is convenient to Capt Bowie he
can send over word what I owe for the butter or include it in one of
the bills for Custis. We all enjoyed the nice ice cream and thank you for
it. Come and see me when you have time.

The signature is quite small because there is no room left on the half sheet of paper on which the note was written. The last word of it is clearly "Lee," and the initial immediately before may be an "M," indicating the note was from Mary Lee, the general's wife rather than the general, which makes more sense considering the invitation to "come see me." The family tradition is that the ice cream was grape-juice sherbet, which is a recipe that has been handed down through my wife's family for generations and which really is quite "nice."

Patty and I not only discovered early on that we loved Civil War history but that we both had ancestors from Virginia. Accordingly, when we married on August 15, 1981, we honeymooned in the Old Dominion State and fell in love with it, surprise, surprise!

We decided to visit our respective ancestral homes, which for her was an imposing mansion named Carysbrook, located near Palmyra, Virginia. Built before the American Revolution, it was supposedly visited by Thomas Jefferson and is still a significant architectural and historic landmark in a historic part of the country.

Concord and Campbell County are not far from there, perhaps fifty miles, but whereas her ancestors were living in the big house, mine were modest tobacco farmers in cabins in a rural setting. All we knew was that my ancestors had moved away from there in 1851, but we stopped at a convenience store and asked if there was anyone named Akers still living in the area. We were directed to a man who told us about a family named Evans living a few miles out of town.

We went to their door and introduced ourselves to Frances Evans, the wife of George Evans. Turned out that a daughter of George Washington Akers had married the grandfather of Mr. Evans, who lived there, making him my third cousin. We talked, feeling right at home, and they invited us to supper. Their children Greg and Ann came over, and we wound up spending the night. To make a long story endless, we became fast friends, as well as family, and Patty and I, over the next few years, purchased ten acres of the old tobacco farm my ancestors left in 1851. The grave of William Akers, who died in 1808, father of John, who married Agnes Bryan, can still be found and recognized in the woods if a person is persistent and gets directions. It is recorded as being the oldest known grave of an Akers in the nation.

My dream is to build a little cabin on that ten acres and have it to retire to or at least spend time at, in a few years. Doing so will sort of complete a small circle within the great circle.

There is more, of course, but the foregoing is more than enough. I cannot imagine bearing up long enough to read similar tales about anybody else's ancestors. The very idea is repugnant.

Postscript

I don't understand why you can't just teach us history
instead of always harping on the past.

GLINDA TO DOCTOR DILLAMOND

in *Wicked,* play based on the novel by Gregory Maguire

FOR ALL THINGS THERE IS A SEASON, AND THE STORIES TOLD HERE HAD theirs, plus some extra.

Otherwise, there is no conclusion. How could there be? History—family, local, national and world—moves forward and on, and we must move with it as long as we can, then enjoy the next great adventure in the great cycle. Perhaps then we'll learn the truth about what really happened, told us by the folks, or spirits, who were there and who know the value of preserving a good tale.

Notes

1. W. Ramsey, ed., *On the Trail of Bonnie and Clyde, Then and Now* (London: Battle of Britain Ltd, 2003), 252.
2. http://redriverhistorian.com/bonnie.html.
3. Henry Kyd Douglas, *I Rode with Stonewall* (Chapel Hill: University of North Carolina Press, 1968), 214–215.
4. Ibid.
5. Louis Burns is listed on the roster of Company D, 11th Illinois Infantry (three-year) regiment, but there is no listing for a Jesse Kulin or Keelin, nor does a soldier of that name appear in any other company of the regiment, and no soldier named Jesse from the regiment is listed as having died on August 4, 1863, although two men of Company K, John Casper and Alexander Lentz, died on that date. It is probable that Jesse belonged to another regiment and that Private Burns was serving as an aide in the post hospital when Jesse died.
6. Monte Akers, "My Darling Charlie," *North South Trader's Civil War Magazine* Vol. XVIII, No. 3 (1991), 18; Marie Melchiori, "The Search for Darling Charlie," Ibid. 23.
7. The newsreel is captured about forty minutes into *Echoes of the Blue and Gray*, Vol. II. It has also been recorded on the Internet and was circulated among members of the Stonewall Brigade re-enactors on their website at www.stonewallbrigade.com/articles_rebelyell.html.
8. It was put on the Internet by the 19th Alabama unit of re-enactors and can be accessed at www.19thalabama.org/favorite. html.

9. E-mail message dated February 14, 2010, from Terryl Elliott to Monte Akers. Terry also compared and analyzed the Alexander and Simmons records as follows: Both the Alexander/WBT and the Simmons/UDC recordings are twenty seconds in length. They each follow the six-part pattern illustrated below of standard short yelps ~ lower, gruffer short yelps ~ short pauses and long pauses.

Legend:

__	standard short yelp
__	lower, gruffer short yelp
- - -	long, three-part yelp
/	short pause
/ /	long pause

Pattern:

Simmons: __ __ - - - / __ __ - - - / / __ __ - - - /

Alexander: __ __ - - - / / __ __ - - - / __ __ - - -

10. *The Handbook of Texas* lists a Henry G. Anderson as having married Carolina Elizabeth Willingham, daughter of Archibald Willingham, probably in Washington County, Texas, circa 1850: www.tshaonline.org/handbook/onlin/articles/ww/kwiif.html; the *Handbook* also reports a Henry Anderson whose family "forted up" with that of Samuel Pierce Newcomb as protection against the Comanches in Stephens County in 1865: www.tashaonline.org/handbook/online/articles/NN/fne33.html.

11. Wallace O. Chariton, *Exploring the Alamo Legends* (Plano TX: Wordware Publishing, 1990), 19.

12. The two are occasionally identified as being the same, including a reference by Chariton, ibid. 29–30, 264.

13. When Texas musician Allen Damron wrote and recorded "Come to the Bower," about the battle of San Jacinto, he selected the name of one of the Tejanos killed at the Alamo to describe as the cousin of the young San Jacinto soldier supposedly singing the song, who is fighting to revenge the death of both father, killed with Fannin, and that cousin. Compounding the error on the cenotaph, he selected the name of Jose Maria Guerrero.

14. Recent information about the Emily West/Emily Morgan story was brought to my attention by Judy Alter, but it was unknown to me at the time I did research for the screenplay. Additional information on the story can be found at www.tamu.edu/ccbn/dewitt/adp/central/warroom/warroom12html and libraries.uta.edu/speccoll/crose05/West.htm.

15. Nobody ever called the 125th anniversary of the Civil War by any other name, probably because it was and is hard to figure out what that name should be. A "quadricentennial" is 400 years, and a "quarter centennial" is only twenty-five

years, so unlike the centennial and probably the future sesquicentennial and bi-centennial, the "quasquicentennial" didn't get called by its proper appellation.

16. http://wesclark.com/jw/reenactors_in_the_attic.html.

17. Inspired by the foregoing, I once wrote a simple set of song lyrics titled "Lee Shall Overcomb," but like the great American classic it parodies, the rhymes and message are not complex and can easily be imagined, so I shall not inflict it on anyone.

18. www.youtube.com/watch?v=WlKc5PapKJc and www.youtube.com/watch?v=MUMa2hHOtc.

19. President's Citation, Medal of Honor present to William Downey, www.homeof heroes.com/moh/citations_1862_cwa/downey.html.

20. Walter F. Beyer and Oscar F. Keydel, eds., *Deeds of Valor*, Vol. I (Detroit: Perrien Keydel, 1901), 349.

21. In fact, he made the list in a 2006 book titled *101 People Who Are Really Screwing America* (New York: Nation Books, 2006); www.amiannoying.com/(S(qyz5qt55xs 5ilvqoix405f45)/collection.aspx?collection=7976 no. 81.

22. A visit to the New York Public Library on January 30, 2010, revealed that the papers of neither William or Charles Cleveland Dodge are deposited there and that they are not listed as being in the collection of any other library, at least according to *The Index of Names in the National Union Catalog of Manuscript Collections, 1959–1984*.

23. www.british_history.ac.uk/report.aspx?compid=75468.

Bibliography

★

BOOKS

Bartlett, John. *Bartlett's Familiar Quotations*. 15th ed. Boston: Little Brown & Co., 1980.

Blanton, DeAnne, and Lauren M. Cook. *They Fought Like Demons: Women Soldiers in the Civil War*. New York: Vintage Books, 2002.

Cassell's History of England, From the Roman Invasion to the War of the Roses, Vol. 1. London: Cassell and Company, Ltd., 1909.

Chariton, Wallace O. *Exploring the Alamo Legends*. Plano TX: Wordware Publishing 1990.

Douglass, Henry Kyd. *I Rode With Stonewall: The War Experiences of the Youngest Member of Jackson's Staff*. Chapel Hill: University of North Carolina Press, 1968.

Elliott, Terryl W. *Dammit, Holler ''em Across: The History of the Rebel Yell*. San Francisco: Partisan Press, 2009.

Farwell, Byron. *Stonewall: A Biography of General Thomas J. Jackson*. New York: W.W. Norton & Co., 1992.

Frost, Lawrence A. *The Custer Album: A Pictorial Biography of General George A. Custer*. Seattle: Superior Publishing Company, 1964.

Fuller, T. A. *The Spear and the Spindle: Ancestors of Sir Francis Bryan (d. 1550)*. Bowie MD: Heritage Books, 1993.

Gilbert, Charles E. . *Flags of Texas*. Gretna LA: Pelican Publishing Co., 1994.

Groneman, Bill. *Alamo Defenders: A Genealogy: The People and their Words*. Austin: Eakin Press, 1990.

Hardorff, Richard G. *Washita Memories: Eyewitness Views of Custer's Attack on Black Kettle's Village*. Norman: University of Oklahoma Press, 2006.

History of Freestone County, Texas. Vol. 1. Fairfield TX: Freestone County Historical Commission, 1978.

Horwitz, Tony. *Confederates in the Attic: Dispatches from the Unfinished Civil War*. New York: Pantheon, 1998.

Huberman, Jack. *101 People Who Are Really Screwing America*. New York: Nation Books, 2006.

Huffines, Alan C. *Blood of Noble Men, The Alamo Siege and Battle: An Illustrated Chronology*. Austin: Eakin Press, 1999.

Kane, Harriett T. *The Gallant Mrs. Stonewall: A Novel Based on the Lives of General and Mrs. Stonewall Jackson*. Larchmont NY: Queens House, 1978.

Leighton, Margaret. *Comanche of the Seventh (A Horse Story)*. New York: Ariel Books, 1957.

Meredith, Roy. *The Face of Robert E. Lee in Life and in Legend*. New York: Fairfax Press, 1981.

Nolan, Alan T. *Lee Considered: General Robert E. Lee and Civil War History*. Chapel Hill: University of North Carolina Press, 1991.

Ramsey, Winston G., ed. *On the Trail of Bonnie and Clyde Then and Now*. London: Battle of Britain International Ltd, 2003.

Sharra, Michael. *The Killer Angels*. New York: Random House, 1974.

Smith, H. Allen. *The Rebel Yell*. Garden City, NY: Doubleday & Co., 1954.

Stern, Phillip Van Doren. *Robert E. Lee: The Man and the Soldier*. New York: McGraw-Hill 1963.

Thompson, John W. *JEB Stuart*. New York: Charles Scribner's Sons, 1930.

Warner, Ezra J. *Generals in Gray*. New Orleans: Lousiana State University Press, 1959.

Watkins, Sam. *Co. Aytch, Maury Grays, First Tennessee Regiment; Or, a Side Show of the Big Show*. Columbia TN: 1882.

PERIODICALS

Akers, Monte. "My Darling Charlie." *North South Trader's Civil War*, XVIII, No. 3 (1991).

———. "That Crazy Cap." *Military Images Magazine* (January–February 1984).

Dew, J. Harvie. "The Yankee and Rebel Yells." *Century Illustrated Magazine*, April 1891, 954–55.

Godfrey, E. S. "Custer's Last Battle." *Century Magazine*, January 1892.

Holzer, Harold, Gabor Boritt, and Mark E. Neely, Jr. "Images of Peace: When it Came to Lee's Surrender, Every Picture Told a Different Story." *Civil War Times*, January 2006, 74–79.

Jones, W.D. "Riding with Bonnie & Clyde." *Playboy*, November 1968.

Kinsolving, Roberta Cary Corbin. "Stonewall Jackson in Winter Quarters: Memories of Moss Neck in the Winter of 1862-63." *Confederate Veteran*, January 1912, 24–26.

Melchiori, Marie. "The Search for Darling Charlie." *North South Trader's Civil War*, XVIII, No. 3 (1991).

Stametelos, James. "Whipple's Patent Military Cap." *Military Images Magazine*, May–June 1984.

U.S. News & World Report, August 15, 1988.

MUSICAL OR OTHER COLLECTIONS

Coleman, William & Carla. *Chantilly Remembrance*. Woodburn OR: Cold Comfort Productions, 1998.

———. *The Haunting War*. Woodburn OR: Cold Comfort Productions, 2005.

———. *The Last Roses*. Woodburn OR: Cold Comfort Productions, 2001.

Horton, Bobby. *Homespun Songs of the C.S.A.*, Vol. 6. Birmingham AL: Bobby Horton, 2001.

The Rebel Yell Lives. Richmond: Museum of the Confederacy, 2008.

RADIO

Radke, Bill, and Amy Scott, hosts, *Weekend America*, June 2, 2007.

INTERNET SITES

Bonnie and Clyde Haunts. http://redriverhistorian.com/bonnie.html

Favorite Things of the 19th Ala. Members. www.19thalabama.org/favorite.html

Medal of Honor Citations. www.homeofheroes.com/moh/citations

Southern Birthright. www.youtube.com/watch?v=WlKc5PapKJc

Southern Birthright. www.youtube.com/watch?v=MUMFa2hHOtc

Ted Turner, et al., at Gettysburg; or, Reenactors in the Attic. http://wesclark.com/jw/reenactors_in_the_attic.html

The Stonewall Brigade (articles). www.stonewallbrigade.com/articles.html

The War Room, Opinion and Debate. "Did the Yellow Rose of Texas really exist or is it just another story from Texas lore?" www.tamu.edu/ccbn/dewitt/adp/central/warroom/warroom12.html

VIDEO

Above the Wind. Atlanta: All Media Inc., 1989.

North and South: The Complete Collection. Warner Brothers DVD, 2004.

MISCELLANEOUS

Jones, Lawrence T. *The Confederate Calendar 2008.* Austin: Confederate Calendar Works, 2007.

Index